keys to art

this book was the idea of
pierre belvès

keys

designed by
marcel jacno

text by
john canaday

to art

captions
and notes by
robert maillard

tudor publishing co
new york

This book was first published, in 1962,
with a French text by Luc Benoist
under the title "Regarde ou les Clefs de l'art"
by Fernand Hazan, publisher, Paris.

English edition first published in 1964
Printed in France

FOREWORD

The simple but ambitious aim of this book is to fill the interval, lengthy or brief according to the individual, that separates the act of seeing and the act of looking. It is through the sight in childhood that we receive the basis of a direct knowledge of the world, a knowledge that education and learning only makes more aware, more thorough and more lucid without effacing the first, fundamental impression.

There is no intention, however, of offering the public another and quite unnecessary history of art, with its welter of erudition and lists of names and dates, and still less a new aesthetic with a novel terminology; it is rather to help the common reader rediscover that hidden power of wonder, which is characteristic of childhood and which awakened in our most distant ancestors a taste for adorning themselves, their homes and places of worship, the pleasure of using a well made tool and the feeling of joy and freedom from looking at a beautiful landscape. In fact, no method can achieve this and it is the aim of this book to revive this profound instinct for beauty without the farrago of learned words, false or even true ideas, and without classifying by schools and giving examples.

If art is in itself a magic way of seeing, it is because the artist has already looked for us. A silent language of forms and objects, its value is so universal that all interpretation obscures it, all words deceive and mislead us. Rilke expressed this perfectly in discussing the mystery of nature: "If a man paints this, it is because he cannot put it into words."

A return to understanding by simply looking, by the direct path of contemplation, that is the true source of every renewal, of every awakening and every miracle. A man looks and the world is reborn.

Sources for color photography are:
A.C.L., Brussels: page 11.—Bibliothèque
Nationale, Paris: 117.—Boitier (Connais-
sance des Arts), Paris: 69.— Dräyer,
Zurich: 91, 130, 139,168 and 171.—Girau-
don, Paris: 105, 147 and 159.—Mayer,
New York: 18.—Meyer, Vienna: 45.—
Millet (Connaissance des Arts), Paris:
183.—Rampazzi, Turin: 57.—Scala,
Florence: 81.
Other photographic credits follow
captions and appear in italics.

CONTENTS

THE reader should notice that this book is called "Keys to Art," not "The Key to Art." If there is anything that can be called the key to art, it is the intuition held intimately at the core of personality, and hence differing, at least slightly, from one person to another. But since this key itself frequently gets locked in, the purpose of this book is to offer a few keys that may be of service in releasing it for use.

The first key, certainly, is to learn to see more than casually. Fixed in our habits, we see little enough of what passes before our eyes every day. We see even less of what a painting, a sculpture, a building, offers us. The routines of daily life condition us to see the practical essentials of things—which is fair enough in a life where coping with practical essentials has to take up most of our time. But paintings and sculptures are not practical essentials. Most buildings are, but the great buildings of all times, even of our own hardheaded time, are also works of art. This means that, like painting and sculpture, they are expressions of the human spirit no matter what practical essentials they

S. Thoby, Rapho. Serge Jacques. Jean Abegg.

also serve, and are subject, like all art, to our habitual blindness.

When habits of seeing the world are used as a way of seeing art, a painting becomes an imitation of something, when it should be instead a revelation. A sculpture is only a more or less pleasing object in stone, bronze or wood, usually a figure of something, when it could be a transfiguration. And buildings, which of all things around us can be most interesting as summaries of a civilization, are reduced to structures occupying certain sites and designed to serve certain purposes, perhaps with certain proportions and embellishments that make them pleasing to the eye.

"Pleasing to the eye" is a dreadful phrase under any circumstances, but is most dreadful of all when applied to a work of art. It implies that art is a soothing optical lotion, and that the way to see art is to let it wash across a surface that has been wearied by more demanding activities. "Stimulating to the eye" would be a little better, indicating that art can jolt us out of habitual ways of seeing, if we will let it. "Challenging to the eye" would be better still, since some effort on our part is necessary if, as a beginning to deeper under-standing, we are ready to see fully.

Compare the way we see with the way we hear. Of all our senses, hearing may be the most subtly attuned. Having learned from experience that a sound once produced is gone immediately, we listen more intently than we look, and may perceive more completely a sound that we hear unexpectedly in a fraction of a moment than we perceive a building we pass every day or a picture that hangs on our wall for years. Nor are we trained to recognize visual devices as we recognize verbal ones. Everyone says, "It wasn't what he said, it was

E. Landau, Rapho.   M. Foucault, Rapho.   Rapho.   Georges Martin, Rapho.

the way he said it," but how many say, "It wasn't what the picture showed, it was the way the artist showed it."

Thus we realize that our enjoyment of a comedian's wit is increased because we can recognize the skill with which he calculates the pause just before his punch line. But few of us are aware of the ways a painter leads us to the climactic point of his picture and emphasizes it by comparable devices. We may admire the rolling cadences of an orator's speech, and miss the sculptor's comparable building up of forms into a unified whole. Consciously we admire the timbre of a great voice, yet we take for granted the texture of a great building.

Of course we are talking here about techniques and materials, which are only the means of art, not its end. The comedian's timing is technique; so is the painter's way of putting a picture together. The orator's rhythms are produced by technique, so are the rhythms of sculptural form; the timbre of a great voice is only raw material that may be used or misused by its owner, and so are the materials in which the architect designs.

If the first key to art is a matter of learning to see such things (and their recognition alone may give much pleasure), it is only the first key of many. For you may say that the effectiveness of a work of art lies not in what the artist says, but in the way he says it, but you cannot say that its greatness lies there. Of course it is what is said that is important or unimportant, true or false, noble or base. The way it is said is simply the effort to reveal as fully as possible the character of the thought. The most obvious truth about art, yet the one least considered by most people, is that if an artist has nothing to say, it makes little difference how great his mastery over the means of saying it, and that no matter how much he may have to say, and no matter how great a man he may be within himself, he is of no consequence as an artist except to the degree that he has mastered the most appropriate way of communicating with the rest of us.

Van Gogh. Boats at Les Saintes-Maries 1888. Private collection.

From this point on, the "appreciation of art"—another deadly phrase, but an irreplaceable one—is a process so complex that it would be discouraging if its rewards did not equal its complexities. Once the first door is opened, any key on the ring will open another. Art is the summary of our history, sometimes in the factual sense as a record of heroes, wars, governments, and the gradual transformation of our planet from a self-contained wilderness to a cosmological speck. But more importantly, art is our history of self discovery. There is nothing anyone can know that does not find its reflection, or better yet its clarification, in art. From superstition to religion, from religion to science, from the way men look to the way they think, it is all there. What we have hoped for, what we have accomplished, where we have failed, what we have believed or doubted, what we have revealed as true or exposed as false, everything that we have found good, true and beautiful or stale, flat and unprofitable, has been expressed in art. Anything we know about anything adds to our understanding of art, and anything we learn from art increases our knowledge of ourselves.

Works of art of any consequence are immortal, but they are not static. They grow even after the civilizations that produced them have died. Nothing is more certain than that a work of art changes from generation to generation and from age to age as the men change who look at it. From the distance of a generation, a century, a millenium, we surely lose something of what the art of the past meant to the men who produced it. But we gain incomparably more than we lose. Because the past produced us stage by stage, and continues to nourish us, we in turn discover within it new meanings extending from, growing upon, the old. Since this is true, some of the ideas propounded in this book might come as surprises to the artists who did the paintings, sculptures and buildings. But if the artists are not here to argue such points, their works are, to offer corroboration or rebuttal. The reader should listen to them. A book on art should be a three sided conversation: the author

Georges Martin, Rapho.   Gorin. Steel sculpture.   Carter, Rapho.   Léger. The Balcony. 1919.

proffers his responses to art, the artist makes them meaningful or invalidates them by the evidence of his work, and the reader takes the two of them on, not as antagonists but as fallible specialists. In disagreements where the decision is close, the benefit of the doubt should go to the artist. He is, after all, the one who counts most. Art cannot be created solely by any set of rules; hence a work of art can be analyzed only up to a point, although the point may be a vantage one for sensing what lies beyond it—the inexplicable something that accounts for the greatness of a great work of art.

I
FIRST KEYS
TO ART

discovering painting

discovering sculpture

discovering architecture

compare, and discover

the pencil as explorer

American. Whistler.
Arrangement in Gray and Black.
Commonly called "Whistler's Mother."
1872. Louvre, Paris.
Giraudon.

Quiet, withdrawn, she sits patiently in a room we know is silent. We see her through her son's eyes ; we recognize and share his tenderness for an individual. But beyond this one woman, beyond this particular room, the artist (rather than the son) tells us of all gentle old age, its resignation, its reflection upon a past where our vitality would be an intrusion.

We call the picture "Whistler's Mother," but the artist's title, "Arrangement in Gray and Black," calls our attention to the aspect of painting least recognized by the average observer—the abstract means an artist uses to translate what he sees into a revelation of what he feels. In "Whistler's Mother" the transforming devices are unusually apparent, but their appropriateness and the finesse of their application sustain the esthetic life of a painting that familiarity should, by now, have reduced to banality. The muted tones, the simplified silhouettes, distill form and color to a point where all agitation, all confusion, is spent. The result could have been only dreary, thin and monotonous if within this reduced world the artist had not played the subtlest variations of light and dark, of shape, and above all of arrangement. The position of the focal point, the head, far to the right and near the top of the picture, is a saving eccentricity. Yet any conspicuous eccentricity would have been fatally disharmonious to the picture's mood. So we are led, without our realizing it, to the secondary focus of the hands, then unobtrusively to the heavy balancing dark mass of the curtain that fills so much of the opposite side. Everything leads our eye in a slow, contemplative movement until we absorb the picture as a whole, but always we return to the beautiful head, which looks away from us, gazes beyond the frame, beyond the room, beyond the world.

Flemish. Bruegel. The Numbering at Bethlehem. 1566. Musées Royaux des Beaux-Arts, Brussels.

Instead of a single figure in the retreat of a closed and quiet room, nearly 200 figures in a busy Flemish village that stretches back across snow and ice into a gray winter sky. Instead of gentle intimacy and secluded revery, all the common pursuits of peasant life. A man butchers a hog while a woman holds a pan to catch blood from the slit throat; children tussle with one another, romp on the ice, spin tops, pull sleds; chickens peck in the snow; birds cut through the sky, and one perches on the tip of a ruined tree; people gossip, gather firewood, build a hut, work at their trades, enter a distant church. In the midst of these usual activities there is an exceptional one, which insistently claims our attention: in the doorway of a decaying building some men sit behind a table, two of them examining a record or dossier of some kind while another, in an opulent furred coat, fills in forms as the villagers crowd around to give

The dark, dominating trunk of this great
tree standing like a barrier between
us and the rest of the picture
is first of all a vertical device
to link earth and sky.
It also accounts for much of the picture's
effect of great depth: the naked
branches enmeshing the scene beyond are
painted with the boldness and clarity
of objects seen at close range,
thus exaggerating the distance of
objects behind them.
And at the same time the
beautiful pattern of winter branches
tells of the tenacious splendor
of a living tree.
A.C.L., *Brussels.*

A villager or two leans against the tree;
others jostle their neighbors and push their way
toward the census takers, who have set
up a table in front of the inn. Some forty
people are gathered in this compact knot and all have come
for the same reason. But each
individual is characterized by his stance,
by his features or expression, by the clothes
he wears. One can almost hear the hubbub
of voices; even the shuffling sound of feet
is evoked by the trampled, once immaculate
carpet of snow.
A.C.L.

In drawing this wooden
framework Bruegel must have experienced
a double pleasure, that of the
creative artist combined with that of
the builder-craftsman. Like the
carpenters he pictures, he, too, builds
a shed, using his skill at perspective
instead of skill with measuring-string
and plumb-line.
As a fellow builder, the artist
catches three workers in typical
gestures, each with his special
tool: saw, gimlet and hatchet.
A.C.L.

A poor hut with a wicker
basket for a chimney; on its roof,
two birds beak to beak; around it,
children playing. A man steps out
of the shed; a peasant woman
in a flat hat of woven straw hoes
her tiny garden still half-hidden
under the snow. A picture within
a picture, telling its own story,
this miniature universe is bound
by a thousand ties, visible and
psychological, to the rest of
the composition.
A.C.L.

Who is this fellow dragging
a long sword and hurrying
across a frozen pond? Where is he
going, and where has he come from?
The story gives no clue,
but the fact of his being placed so
conspicuously in the forefront of the
picture and in the right-
hand corner, as if he had just this
moment entered it, is too
telling to be uncalculated.
Perhaps the artist wanted to let us know
that the scene we are looking in on is
not limited to what he has shown us,
but is all of a piece with the rest of
a world that extends beyond the borders
of the canvas. A.C.L.

the required information. We may not at first attach unusual importance to a woman mounted on a donkey who seems to protect something beneath her cloak while a man, bending forward under his burden, leads the way through the unnoticing village.

In this full pattern, each detail is a pattern in itself, sometimes curious, sometimes even grotesque, always charged with life . Each figure, each building, each tree, each of the wheels that are scattered from foreground to background in a pattern-within-a-pattern, is a triumph of design when taken singly. But the artist's staggering feat is to have unified so many hundreds of elements into a whole that fuses two apparently incompatible pictures: he tells us of the random bustle, the unplanned movement in a scattered and haphazard village landscape ; at the same time, he fits these random elements into a composition so neatly constructed, so beautifully controlled, that the longer we examine it as an abstract arrangement the less we can imagine modifying any part without disrupting the whole.

Another thing: since the picture is called "The Numbering at Bethlehem," more than description and composition must be involved. A story, surely ; is there also a comment? The numbering was the census that brought Mary and Joseph to Bethlehem, and a prelude to the massacre of the innocents, when Herod ordered the murder of newborn boys in order to do away with the one who, by prophecy, was to be king of the Jews.

Bruegel had an immediate reason for laying the scene in the kind of Flemish village he and his contemporaries knew. Thus, as in the companion "Massacre of the Innocents," he comments through the disguise of a Biblical subject on Spanish persecutions in Flanders. The officials and later the murdering soldiers enter the village with the foreign authority and the cruelty to which the country was subjected. But even if we forget the topical reference, the transference of locale from ancient Judea to Bruegel's home ground brings the story into an area that was his own in more than a geographical sense.

Bruegel discovered for painting the zest and humor of the common man who shares the soil's plainness but also its vitality and perpetual renewal. Mary and Joseph enter Bruegel's village as anonymously as they entered

Bethlehem. They are bound into the pattern of other common, anonymous people who go about their work unnoticing. But Bruegel points them out to us by placing them where, once we have seen them, we cannot forget them, and now we know what the treasure is that the woman protects not only beneath her cloak but within her body. We become secret participants in a story more miraculous for being invisible to other witnesses in the broad light and the commonplace surroundings of everyday. We realize, too, that everywhere the everyday is only a surface that conceals an eternal miracle.

Italian. Masaccio.
The Tribute Money. 1426-1428.
Fresco in the Brancacci Chapel,
Santa Maria del Carmine, Florence.
The gospel according to
Saint Matthew tells
us that Jesus, when he was
rejected in Nazareth, went to
live and teach in Capernaum.
This settlement on the Sea of
Galilee was a commercial and
customs center and exacted an
entrance toll. When a Roman
official insisted on payment
of two drachmas fee for right of
entry, Jesus told Peter to go and
extract it from a gullet of a fish.

The forms in "Whistler's Mother" may be read as virtually flat silhouettes. Those in
"The Numbering at Bethlehem" are enchanting as silhouettes but tell fully only when
read simultaneously as solid forms in a deep stage. "The Tribute Money," at the far end
of this scale, is fully comprehensible only when its forms are read as volumes interrelated
to one another and to the space they occupy. A figure excised from its context with other
figures and with the accompanying landscape or architecture (as at upper right) is like

16

Conforming to the medieval theater idea of representing different scenes of action, perhaps far apart, on the same stage, the artist was not bound to respect a logical sequence of events. This picture should be read as follows:
in the center, Christ and His disciples with the official who is demanding the toll; at the left, the miracle of the two drachmas; at the right, the payment of the tribute. The simultaneity of events results in Saint Peter being represented three times and the official twice.

an amputated limb: its shape is unchanged and its function remains apparent, but its life is gone and it can only echo inertly the reasons for being it once had as part of an integrated system. The breadth and amplitude of this system, united by dignity of gesture and solemnity of gaze, give the static masses a stately processional quality and account for the majesty of a painting which in lesser hands could have turned out to be only a bit of anecdotal narration.

17

Spanish. Picasso.
Woman with a Fan. 1905.
Mrs. Averell Harriman
Collection, New York.

A work of art need not have a precisely definable subject. It may draw instead on the uncharted network of associations stirred by a riddle and on the even more subtle associations stirred by pure color and pure form. The gesture of Picasso's enigmatic woman with a fan has been called a 20th century echo of the Angel Gabriel's hieratic greeting to the Virgin Mary in medieval annunciations. It can suggest also a more mundane gesture of farewell to an unseen friend. But the picture may be most satisfying when least specifically explained.

Discovering sculpture

Great art is a process of transformation by which images of even the most familiar things become revelational, by which eternal themes are renewed by restatement in terms peculiar to the artist and his time. But there is another kind of transformation to which this revelation is subject, the transformation of inert matter, whether it is paint, stone, wood, clay or metal, into images that have their own life.

Paint may be turned into images of things fluid, vaporous or firm, may take on the glow and warmth of flesh or the solidity of earth, may even become sunlight striking through the air of the countryside and yet not lose its identity as paint, as an expertly manipulated layer of fatty richness on canvas or a transparent film of color over paper. Paint is an obliging medium, quick to yield to whatever demands a skilled artist makes of it, ready to assume whatever form, whatever texture, whatever weight, whatever nature, the image requires.

But the sculptor's materials defeat him if he pushes them far beyond their natural character. Much of the beauty of stone sculpture is that it remains stone. The grain and texture of wood remain a part of whatever is carved in it. Flesh, drapery or foliage cast in bronze must accept the character of bronze first, and that of flesh, drapery or foliage second. A sculptor's problem is to accede to his material's demand that it be recognized for itself, yet to see that it does not interpose itself between him and us. As compensation, his materials offer him their own beauty as an integral part of his creation if he can control them without violating them. An even greater compensation is the force, the decisiveness, inherent in sculpture's physical existence as a three dimensional reality. Painting may offer us an illusion to accept or reject, but sculpture is indisputably a tangible presence, demanding a recognition we are incapable of denying. That may be why bad sculpture is so emphatically bad. It is certainly a reason why great sculpture imposes itself on our consciousness with such power. The danger is that sculpture's extraordinary reality often deceives the careless eye into regarding it as an imitation of nature, so that the sculptor's interpretative transformation is sacrificed. Verrocchio's "David" exemplifies this truth. It transmutes an acute anatomical study into the apotheosis of vigor with elegance.

When Verrocchio studied with Donatello, to whom he is indebted as a sculptor, he was already well known as a goldsmith. His goldsmith's talent for elaborate design meticulously executed is evident here and accounts for much of the effect of elegance in a sculpture that, over-all, is remarkable for its vigor. Hebraic motifs are chased at the borders of the cuirass and on the hem of the tunic, but the springing locks framing the sensitive face are equally, if less noticeably, designed with the precision of a small, precious ornamental object. *Brogi-Giraudon.*

Discovering sculpture

Italian. Verrocchio. David. Bronze. 1476. Museo Nazionale (Bargello), Florence. — This earliest of known statues by the artist was commissioned by Lorenzo de' Medici, who made a gift of it to the Signoria of Florence. Its position of honor at the head of the main stairway in the Palazzo Vecchio was ill-chosen because the figure could not be seen from all sides as the artist planned it to be. Verrocchio sculptured the severed head of Goliath as a pedestal base and the boy stands provocatively astride it, at once victorious and at ease. Any suggestion of violence or brutality is contradicted by the disarming immature grace of the model. Finally, so convincingly natural is his attitude that one is hardly aware of the adroit asymmetry of the two arms.

A winged goddess of victory alighting on the prow of a warship, the personification of jubilant power and rushing pride, a magnificent stone that seems molded by the air into which it thrusts, balancing itself against the motion of the sea. More fortunate than most sculptures held captive in museums, the Nike of Samothrace is installed at the top of a giant flight of steps in the Louvre, a far way from the rocky headlands of her island and robbed of the brilliant, changing light of the Greek sun, but still free enough.

André Vigneau, Paris.

Technically the "Winged Victory" stands at the danger point of tour-de-force; conceptually, at the brink of melodrama. But it does not teeter. With almost arrogant assurance it achieves the impossible, combining the serenity of Greek sculpture's golden age with the theatricalism of its decline. In abstract essence it is a design that traces the gigantic rhythms of the body and elaborates them by clinging and flying drapery which, realistic in effect, is actually an arbitrary, even an abstract, sculptural pattern.

The sculptures here, bronze plaques from the doors of the church of San Zeno in Verona, have little in common with Verrocchio's Renaissance youth or the anonymous Greek master's winged goddess, except the quality of greatness that unites all three as expressions of contrasting civilizations.

An immediately apparent difference is that plaques, like paintings, are limited by borders and must be seen frontally. Bas-relief sculpture is neither two-dimensional like painting nor fully three-dimensional. In what might be called its two-and-a-half dimensions, its volume and depth combine sculptural modeling with what is essentially drawing. Some bas-reliefs open deep backgrounds through illusionistic perspective in relief so low that it becomes little more than line. Such highly developed devices were unknown to the early medieval sculptors of San Zeno, but ignorance of technical sophistications is an appropriate corollary to unquestioning acceptance of the supernatural. These Biblical and evangelical scenes have the immediate force of literal belief, while for us, paradoxically, they also take on the quality of fantasy precisely because they are separated from the mundane literalism of "correct" representation, a response that is valid on our part even though it would have puzzled the sculptors. We share so little of their faith, that their art enriches us less by inviting our participation than by permitting us to examine from a distance a vision we have lost.

As designers, the San Zeno sculptors faced the narrator's problem of defining a place, populating it with characters engaged in frequently complicated activities, and of doing so within set dimensions. The problems are solved with ingenuity, often with wit, and always with conviction.

Romanesque. Details of bronzes on the doors of the church of San Zeno in Verona. 11th-13th centuries. From left to right: the Flight into Egypt, the Entry of Christ into Jerusalem, the Last Supper, the Arrest of Christ.—The Crucifixion, the Last Judgment, Salome's Dance before Herod, Adam and Eve Cast Out of Paradise.—Adam and Eve Condemned to Work, the Dove Bringing an Olive Branch to Noah, Mask of a Lion, Moses Receiving the Tablets of the Law.—The Prophet Balaam, San Zeno Fishing, the Carter Possessed of a Demon, the Building of Noah's Ark. *Walter Dräger.*

Saint Etienne,
patron of the cathedral
at Bourges.
Jacques Boulas.

Architecture is the all-embracing art, the art that stands alone in being imperatively demanded by society, the only art that serves practical necessity yet the one that most inclusively catalogues the ideals of its society. In one way it is the least personal of the arts, since the architect must think first of the needs of others and only secondarily, if at all, of himself as an artist with the privilege of self-expression. Yet if architecture is the least personal art for the man who practices it, there is no other art that more intimately affects so many people. Because a building must be planned to fulfill a social function and can be brought into existence only through the mechanics of construction, an architect must be part informal sociologist and part engineer if his work is to be good. He must also be an artist if his work is to be great.

All artists are channels through whom the thought and the spirit of an age is directed, refined and recorded, but the painter and the sculptor are more free than the architect to exploit the fancies of a special group or an individual, and thus sometimes they leave records of eccentricities that concentrate the special flavor of a limited time and place. Such opportunities may also be offered the architect now and then; the history of fanciful and specialized architecture is just as fascinating as the history of fanciful and specialized painting in its recall of the curious ways some men have found to divert themselves or the odd directions they have explored in attempts to fulfill themselves. But the greatest buildings of the world have been commissioned as appropriate shelters and settings for the activities most closely connected with the spirit that dominates an age, whether it is the worship of a god, which demands a temple, the imposition of power, which demands a palace, or a preoccupation with the making of money, which demands a skyscraper. Among these, the most complicated and complete summary of man's life, hopes, and fears in any age is the Gothic cathedral.

Façade and towers of
Saint Etienne de Bourges, one of the
six great Gothic cathedrals of France.
Jacques Boulas.

Saint Etienne de Bourges. The west front. Owing to a somewhat exceptional scheme (seen also in adaptations at Burgos and Toledo) this façade has five portals giving entrance to the nave and double side aisles. In the center, the portal of the Last Judgment; on the left, those of Saint Guillaume, the bishop-founder of the church, and of the Virgin; on the right, the portals of Saint Etienne and of Saint Ursine, the first bishop of Bourges. Another particularity: Bourges is one of the few Gothic cathedrals whose plan does not take the form of the cross; it has no transept and the nave extends without interruption from the entrance to the choir.
Jacques Boulas.

Discovering architecture

Sculpture, never more closely bound to architecture than here, made the cathedral an encyclopedia illustrating the history and science of the world as men knew it, and the life of men in the world as they saw it around them, and the morality of the world in its position as proving ground between heaven and hell. Painting, dematerialized as colored light, has never reached so close an identification with celestial mysteries as in the cathedral's stained glass windows. With music and drama serving the celebration of the Mass, the fusion of the arts was complete. But it was architecture, unsurpassed in its combination of structural daring and spiritual aspiration fully realized, that absorbed the other arts into itself to create on earth a house of God that proved the divinity of our yearning to cast off the limitations of the flesh and to verify the existence of the soul.

The medieval passion for symbolism catalogued every facet of the universe into a system of Christian theology. Scientific fact and fantastic legend were equally adaptable as ramifications from the unquestionable central truth of the world as God's creation, of man as a kind of dearly beloved problem child, and of Christ as God's intermediary. Ancient pagan philosophy was interpreted to fit neatly into a plan that accommodated all history past, current and future. In this arbitrary scheme the difference between naive popular superstition and sophisticated theological manipulation was sometimes only the difference between simplicity and elaboration, but no conclusion could seem false or forced when it supported the central premise that God existed, a premise accepted with a faith so strong that to subject it to proof by logic was only to declare one's confidence in its invulnerability. Churchmen planned the sculpture of the cathedral to summarize their conclusions, but the architect-as-builder surpassed the theologian as the spokesman of his age. His incredible structures gave stone a life that soared heavenward, the triumph of spirituality over materiality. The perfect logic of his engineering created a vibrant, hovering space that remains man's supreme expression of the mystery of God.

New York: Manhattan's skyscrapers seen from Brooklyn Bridge.
Goldman, Rapho.

Arles: aerial view. The amphitheater and theater, both Roman
Archives photographiques, Paris.

The total work of architecture is not a single building, but the city. Even the Gothic cathedral, so nearly complete within itself, takes on its full meaning only when it rises above the clustering town that it blesses, and which in turn sends through it the sustaining flow of life.

The city is a spontaneous growth, only partially controllable, that develops its height, its breadth, its pattern, like a plant with the power of adjusting its character to changing conditions as it grows. The impress of its finest days may remain visible in an old city beneath the overlay of centuries. Arles was once the handsomest city in ancient Gaul, and from the air today its Roman past still dominates its inglorious present as an undistinguished provincial market town.

Whether they are ugly or beautiful, the individual buildings of New York City are lost in the spectacle of its skyline, the crowning architectural achievement of the twentieth century. This architecture-in-the-mass has determined its own form by satisfying the economic demands of a vast city crowded onto a relatively small island, rising highest where most powerfully forced upward by the impossibility of growing outward. The soaring lift of the Gothic cathedral was not a matter of practical necessity but of spiritual expression. Practical necessity and the unspiritual stimulation of commerce lifted the New York skyscrapers even higher. But in the process that forced the skyscraper into being, a kind of purification has taken place. The century's vigor, its inventiveness, its refusal to acknowledge limitations to its powers, are almost literally raised above the base uses to which it has put those powers.

But for all its vitality, this growth is determined by demands of the moment, often to the embarrassment of the future. We are learning that architects must design not only buildings, but also the cities that hold them. Rising in Brazil is a city planned in its totality on a site where no buildings existed. Partially finished, it offers some spectacular structures which, although in use, refuse to come alive. Eventually Brasilia may prove that a city may be conceived as a total architectural unit, or it may prove that we can only modify a natural, rank and wonderful growth as watchful observers of the patterns cities set for themselves.

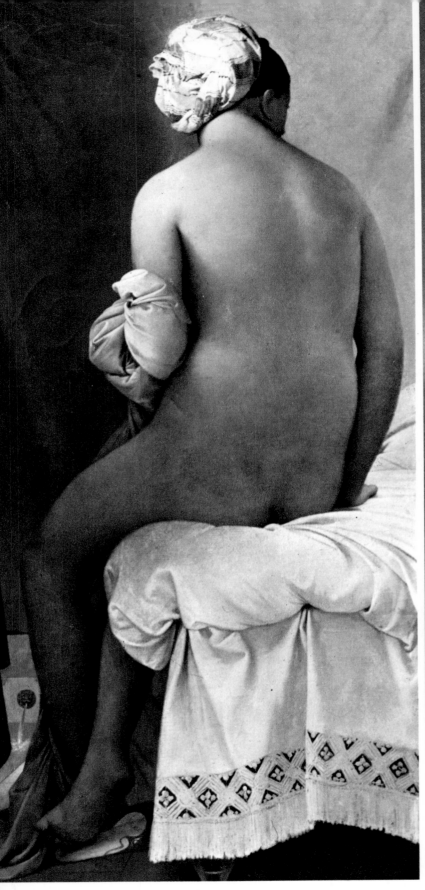

French. Ingres. The Bather of Valpinçon (detail). 1808. Louvre, Paris.—An idolator of sensuous feminine beauty, Ingres was, contradictorily, the dominant spirit of a pedantic Academy dictating a sterile formula that should have reduced his art to tiny exercises. The implacably defined contours, the enamel-like surface, respect the formulas he dictated. But his mastery of line turns the contours into poetic arabesques, and his tightly controlled brush is a discipline, but not a defeat, for his vibrant sensuality. The rarefied air of French neo-classicism made many painters its victims; Ingres remained, in spite of himself, its supreme master. *Giraudon.*

Hindu. Vrikshaka . 10th century. Archeological Museum, Gwalior Fort, Madhya Bharat.—Hindu art, a religious one, is free of the dilemma, present in Western art, of reconciling ideal and real, spirit and matter. The Hindu sees natural form in a context of cosmic forces and believes that it is touched by the divine. The human form is the most often used as the most expressive one to represent mysteries that can be symbolized but not explained. Hamadryads in female form personify the supernatural force that makes a tree or a forest seem alive. The lotus eyes, the twist of the body, the heavy breasts, the wasp waist, are ritualistic conventions. *Drayer.*

Hindu. Lakshmi. Deccan, Southern ndia. 13th century. Musée Guimet, Paris. This bronze has shapes and a rhythm familiar to us after seeing an example of Hindu art in the statue of Vrikshaka. We are three centuries beyond. Recognizing the same motifs makes us aware of the continuity of a tradition. Lakshmi, goddess of beauty and prosperity, rose, like Venus, out of the sea, a lotus in her hand. She was traditionally represented with a pale face, round breasts, a slender waist and blue arms and thighs. A far remove from naturalism, the style follows ritual rules observed in gestures and postures of ceremonial temple dancers today. *Giraudon.*

French. Jacques Lipchitz (born in Lithuania). Seated Woman. 1917. Private collection.—If one can ignore preconceived ideas about contemporary sculpture while looking at this example of it, one can find a not too far-fetched resemblance to the type of idol archeologists unearth in the Middle East. One finds no symbolism, however, in this assemblage of components of the human body, and the distortions have no sacred function. They serve an allusive geometry, an investigation of relations and properties, lines, surfaces and angles. The body serves only as a point of departure for the construction of a new object with a life of its own. *Marc Vaux.*

The pencil as explorer

For anyone who can manage a pencil, the effort to copy a work of art is a good auxiliary discipline in studying it. The hand, less facile than the eye, checks the eye's cursory survey and forces it to look again at lines, contours, masses, and their interrelationships. What accounts for the sense of quivering life relayed to us by Dürer's famous drawing of a hare? How is the acutely observed and precisely recorded detail bound into such a compact structure? Contrasts are everywhere within this perfect unity: the tense, springy whiskers and the soft fur; the bright, glittering eye and the blunt nose; the long, curling ears sprouting from the small, chunky head. The whiskers, which we may notice with appreciative pleasure and then pass by, are a complicated spray of microscopically tapered lines. Occasionally one of them runs a bit askew, varying what might otherwise have been too mechanical a scheme. The quality of such details is so dependent on Dürer's hand that even the most accurate copy would be, to an expert, a kind of forged signature. But these details compose, rather than lie upon, the tensely bunched masses of the body. Dürer's genius as a draughtsman was that his eye perceived and his hand recorded the broad totality of an object with its expressive minutiae.

Spanish. Goya.
Young Hare (after Dürer).
Goya was an admirer of Rembrandt
but he now and then shows himself
curious, at least, about
the precision and objectivity
he found in work by Dürer, a genius
differently endowed. His copy
is as carefully drawn as the model.
Even so, it has a warmth not at all
typical of the German master.
Goya disdains the obligation to delineate
each separate hair.
Instead he clothes the animal
in a coat of fur to which he enjoys
giving a silken sheen.
Bulloz.

Often inspired by Dürer,
Hans Hoffmann was a
contemporary whose favorite
subjects were insects and
flowers. Alongside is his
copy of the famous "Hare.'
He couched it in a botanical
setting, this, too, borrowed
from a watercolor by Dürer.
Anderson-Giraudon.

German. Dürer. Young Hare. 1502. Watercolor and
gouache. Albertina, Vienna.—A man of the
Renaissance, Dürer craved beauty and hunted
rational principles. He investigated
perspective and human and animal proportions
with the insatiable curiosity and the scientist-
minded conscientiousness that led him to
acute observations of microscopically
minute details in nature. He was a mystic
who theorized about God's relation to a
wondrous world and to his own ability
to create. He was a simple man,
extraordinarily complex.

45

Indo-Persian.
The Shah Jahan, miniature from the beginning of the 17th century.
Schönbrunn Palace. Austria.

Dutch. Rembrandt. Copy of the "Shah Jahan." 1652-1655. Cabinet des Dessins, Louvre, Paris.—Perching the hawk not on the right wrist of the horseman where it belongs but on the left one, Rembrandt has intentionally committed a technical error which the falconer would not condone. His interest is in making the most of an ornamental pattern by extending it into unused space ,not in following rules and making an exact copy. *Archives photographiques, Paris.*

Italian. Raphael. Portrait of Balthazar Castiglione. 1516-1519. Louvre, Paris. *Giraudon.*

Flemish. Rubens. Copy of the central portion of the "Battle of Anghiari" by Leonardo da Vinci. Louvre, Paris.—In 1503 the city of Florence commissioned Leonardo to do a fresco for the Great Council Hall of the Palazzo Vecchio. There were some 26×66 feet of wall space to be covered and the patriotic subject was assigned: the battle at Anghiari in 1448 in which the Florentines defeated the Milanese. Leonardo finished the preliminary cartoon in 1505. He started work on the actual wall but interrupted it the following year to go to Milan and never managed to get back to finish the job.
Fifty years later a new commission had Vasari redoing the wall. The best record we have of Leonardo's intention was made by Rubens and is illustrated here. This could be a copy of Leonardo's preliminary sketch, which was on exhibition for a long time and was eagerly studied by the many artists who came to see it, or may be derived from a small version of the sketch that Leonardo also made. It touches us to know that Vasari, who was required to cover over the start Leonardo had made on his fresco, left a painstakingly exact description of it. *Giraudon.*

46

Sketch of the "Balthazar Castiglione" by Rembrandt.
1639. Albertina, Vienna. *Museum photograph.*

Copy of the "Balthazar Castiglione" by Matisse.
About 1894. Musée de Bagnols-sur-Cèze.

The pencil as explorer

In the early and affluent years of his career Rembrandt was an enthusiastic collector of works of art. His taste ranged from Van Eyck and Quentin Metsys to Raphael and Giorgione and he had masterpieces by these painters in his fine house alongside notable pieces of antique sculpture. Because he was a collector he went to auctions; because he was an artist he could bring home something even on occasions when he was outbid: a souvenir in the form of a hasty sketch, like the remarkable one here, of a work he had admired. There is a world of difference between Rembrandt's shorthand reminder and the free but painstaking copy of the portrait which Matisse made in the Louvre when he was about 25 years old. It is evidence of how respectfully, zealously and profoundly Matisse studied the old masters. It is also a lesson in humility taught by a young artist who would make his own mark as a master in his own times.

Spanish. Picasso. Wash drawing after the panel by Altdorfer. 1953—
Picasso is always surprising. How cavalier he seems at first glance about faithfulness to the Altdorfer original in view of the fact that he chose it to study. On looking more carefully—we are learning from him already—we discover that not only has he respected innumerable details but, more important, he has analyzed the work, stripping it to essentials, bringing us closer and closer to what makes it live.

German. Altdorfer.
The Shrouding of Saint Sebastian. 1518.
Germanisches Museum, Nuremberg.

Hubert and Jan van Eyck. Adoration of the Lamb, part of the Ghent Altarpiece.

Michelangelo.
Madonna.

Roman mosaic.
Museo Nazionale, Naples.

Toulouse-Lautrec.
La Goulue. Louvre, Paris.

Of the eight works reproduced here, only three are still where they were originally, still serving the purpose for which they were made. The van Eycks' "Adoration of the Lamb" has always been in the Cathedral of Saint Bavon in Ghent, the central panel in the lower tier of a polyptychal altarpiece in the chapel of Burgomaster Josse Vydt, who paid 600 crowns for it. The "Madonna" by Michelangelo has stayed where it was placed by Flemish merchants who gave it to the church of Notre Dame in Bruges. To see Fra Angelico's fresco one still visits the ninth cell of the monastery of San Marco in Florence, now a museum.

The other masterpieces are exiles. The horse's head comes from the east pediment of the Parthenon. Mantegna's "Madonna of Victory" was once enthroned on the high altar of Santa Maria della Vittoria, a church at Fornova, to commemorate the battle which Gianfrancesco Gonzaga claimed to have won over Charles VIII in 1945. Lautrec's canvas decorated a booth at the "Foire du Trône". As for the Roman mosaic, it once graced a rich man's house in Pompei. No one knows where the tetrarch group came from or was first seen.

Greek. Horse of Selene.
British Museum, London.

Fra Angelico.
Coronation of the Virgin.

Mantegna. Madonna of Victory
Louvres, Paris.

Roman.
Group of tetrarchs.

II

WORKS OF ART
AND THEIR SOURCES

art and magic

art and the gods

the life of the grave

heroes

the great commissions

the new maecenas

the artist witness of his time

the artist as soliloquist

Prehistoric. Ivory head, called the "Dame de Brassempouy" (Landes) Height, about one inch. Aurignacian period. Musée de Saint-Germain-en-Laye. *Giraudon.*

Ranged along the walls of museums, sometimes ill-displayed like objects in storage, sometimes over-dramatized like expensive merchandise for sale, the art of the ancient past seems ready to speak to us. Mute, an exile in time, it has survived the forces that generated it, the society that needed it. An exile in place, it stands in the hall of an institution, a document for preservation instead of a living part of a temple, a palace, or a monument dedicated to gods or men we have never known, have forgotten, or do not understand. When it is very old, it may be the only record of its past except for a few bones. It has survived by chance more often than not, although sometimes it has been saved from destruction because it interested somebody as a curiosity or a souvenir. Even its final enshrinement as art may be a kind of deformation, since we look at it as something to be enjoyed by one esthetic standard or another, forgetting or not knowing that its esthetic function was secondary, at best, to a vanished primary one.

Of course the objects in museums are enjoyable purely as works of art, but the more ancient they are, the less we understand them if that is the limit of our enjoyment. Art for art's sake is a modern idea. Art began as an instrument of ritual, celebration and sorcery, invested with powers to invoke or placate unseen beings, and to exert magical controls over known ones. Beautiful and strange, these sculptures or paintings from a culture so radically foreign to our own may stir in us, even now, a fuzzy, half-recognized echo of the response they stirred so powerfully so long ago. But in a picture-glutted age, we cannot imagine the potency held by carved or painted images in the mind of prehistoric men, or even of any other men who lived before the photograph and the printing press surrounded us by thousands, tens of thousands, millions of pictures of everything. The extraordinary thing is that even now pictures can pull at us so strongly. It is almost impossible not to look at a picture, even if it is a cheap advertisement and even though we may dismiss it immediately. In its weakest form, an image today still has this vestigial magical strength, and we admit the sorcery of inert representations of living things by such phrases as ''a speaking likeness,'' recognizing a degree of witchcraft in something that no amount of familiarity can make entirely prosaic.

From prehistoric times when such a word as ''esthetics'' could not have existed, we have to trace forward a very long way before painting and sculpture, even in the service of magic's less superstitious and more philosophical sister, religion, relinquish their incantational function to a purely esthetic one, and perhaps this relinquishment is never complete. Certainly in the middle ages the statues of the virgin were more than embodiments of an ideal. For most people they were more nearly the materialization of the Virgin herself, accounting for hundreds of stories about statues that moved and spoke on special occasions. Art has always been and still is part of our effort to discover our place in the scheme of things, to explore and control the universe we live in. Even today when this is done so spectacularly by science, the artist still explores within himself as a proxy for the rest of us. When we speak of art as a release, and no matter how much we may also speak of art for art's sake, we mean that the artist is invoking whatever he most venerates, exorcizing whatever personal devils most torture him, finding a private magic in art which began, perhaps as much as 30,000 years ago, as the magic of the tribe.

This tribal magic was performed in caves that were reserved as places of sacred ritual. Their walls and ceilings swarmed with images of bison and deer,

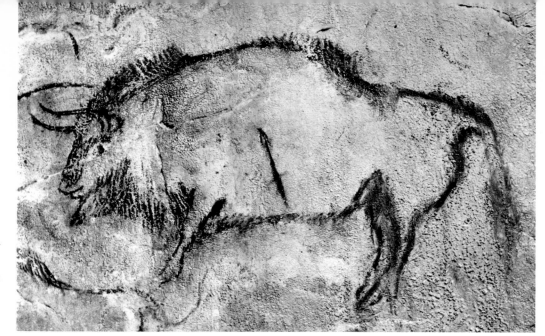

Prehistoric.
Bison wounded by arrows.
Grotte de Niaux (Ariège).
Magdalenian period, about
12,000 B.C.   Yan, Rapho.

the animals most hunted. Magnificent as works of art by our standards, these paintings by primitive men capture the essence of the imaged creatures with an economy remindful of the refinements of sophisticated art. For the cave man this capture was all but literal. The idea that unites a total being to his outward appearance, that makes the soul the inhabitant of the flesh, identified the image with the animal itself. By materializing the animal's soul, men held it within their power. They gained control over it in the hunt and, by representing it pregnant, assured the fecundity of a creature that must continue to reproduce itself for the survival of the tribe. What happened to these tribes we cannot know, but they survived in a way they had not planned: their presence is impressively evoked in their painted caves.

Hunting scene.
Wall painting. Spain.

Prehistoric.
Bison carved in reindeer horn.
From the Grotte de la Madeleine
(Dordogne). About 15,000 B.C.
Musée de Saint-Germain-en-Laye.
Archives photographiques, Paris.

52

Art and magic

Examples of
prehistoric tools:
Left, bay leaf-shaped cutter.
Solutrean period. Musée de Saint-
Germain-en-Laye.—Used as a knife or as
a tip for spears or lances. *Giraudon.*

Right, flint pick carved on both faces.
Acheulian period.
Musée de l'Homme, Paris.
Attached to a handle or simply
held in the hand. *Giraudon.*

Egyptian. Bird-headed deity.
Painted terra cotta. Early Predynastic,
about 4000 B.C. Brooklyn Museum.
A bird representing the spirit of the
dead whether man or woman was always
female. The beaked head, suggesting
a flying bird, and the upraised arms,
unusual in Egyptian art, lead to the
surmise that the deity had to do with
the uplifting of the soul, with an idea
of resurrection, and served the
function of assuring that the spirit of
the deceased person would survive.
Museum photograph.

Art and magic

Egyptian. The Rite of the Opening of the Mouth. Tomb of Inherka, Thebes. About 1200 B.C.—Anubis, god of the necropolis, presents the mummy of the deceased with a flask of perfume. *Hassia.*

Egyptian. Ma'y and his wife at a funeral banquet. Tomb of Ramose, Thebes. About 1400 B.C.

Egyptian. Nakht and his wife
in adoration before Osiris and
Ma'at. Papyrus of
the XVIII Dynasty.
British Museum, London.
Museum photograph.

Prehistory merges gradually into history; nomadic hunters are replaced by a sedentary people who cultivate the land and build cities; superstition gives way to religion; hope and fear, which mean life and death, are examined and formulated into a code to perpetuate existence and defeat the void; in the service of this code, and this civilization, art as sorcery merges into an art where the magical function is retained in forms also designed to give esthetic delight. Egypt is born.

It was a civilization obsessed with a need for physical permanence, haunted by the idea that the soul, in its next life, remains dependent upon its physical house, the body, for shelter. The Egyptians could not concede that the soul might die with the body, but neither could they accept its release as total. Future life was so firmly knit to earthly life, in a scheme so satisfactory to the Pharaohs, who were both gods and kings, that the passion for eternity in the next world included dogmatic prohibitions against change in this one.

In this most static of civilizations over thousands of years art served as record keeper and intermediary with the supernatural. Because mummified bodies might be lost or destroyed, statues by the thousands were carved as acceptable substitute refuges for the soul. And by the thousands these sculp-

55

Art and magic

tures are often dry and repetitious, created on formulas imposed by a religion that made any departure from the status quo a heresy. But the rigid, repetitious forms of Egyptian art represent no limitations inherent in the Egyptian artist; rather, his genius is apparent wherever life suffuses an art forced to concern itself so ritualistically with death.

The soul did not journey alone. It went equipped with all the appurtenances of earthly life, and these were supplied by sculptures and paintings in the tombs. Here the rules were less restricting, or their violations less serious, and the artists showed with tremendous verve everything from ploughmen in the fields, bakers at their ovens and boatmen on the Nile, to lovers, hunting companions, pet birds and animals, musicians, dancers, and all the other paraphernalia of sports, games, amusements and fashionable toilette. Such warm and sprightly company indicates that life in ancient Egypt, at least as led by the privileged, was good enough to explain the strong reluctance to leave it, and to tie firmly, forever, to the wonderful world of earth.

How secure they made this bond is apparent in the tombs at Thebes. As in the small chambers of the tomb of Nakht, who was an official in the service of the Pharaoh, their lives are perpetuated felicitously. Nakht's banquets are spread; his garden flourishes around his pool; his servants are busily at work; he and his wife regard one another with affection. Even the gods, accepting gifts and adoration from these happy people, seem more gracious than in their more formal dealings with the Pharaohs in the temples.

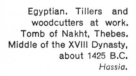

Egyptian. Tillers and woodcutters at work. Tomb of Nakht, Thebes. Middle of the XVIII Dynasty, about 1425 B.C. *Hassia.*

Egyptian. Statue of Kha, Chief of the
Great Place. Wood. About 1450-1375 B.C.
Museo Egizio, Turin.—Egyptian
civilization is matched by no other
in its elaborate use of art to
assure its dead a magic survival in
an afterlife. Surviving for us in
this effective "double" is an
official (he could be called an
architect) charged with the fitting
out of the tomb of Tuthmosis IV in
the Valley of the Kings. We know
more about this important but relatively
modest functionary than we will
probably ever know about illustrious
personages in Chaldean or
Assyrian history. The figure was
found in a tomb at Deir el Medineh
standing over a quantity of objects
and provisions stockpiled to supply
the deceased with all that he had
enjoyed in life and everything he
might need in the hereafter: furniture,
clothing, food of all sorts and, of
course, indispensable work tools—
scribe's tablets, mason's level, ruler.
An unexpected addition to the
necessities was a mineral collection
the deceased had cherished in his
lifetime. The garlands of lotus, still
intact, that adorn the statue are the
very ones placed there
on the funeral day.

57

The god Bel, flanked by two
Palmyra divinities in Roman
military dress. 1st century A.D.
Louvre, Paris. *Archives photographiques.*

Roman. Monumental archway and ruins
of the great colonnade approach to
the temple of Bel at Palmyra (Syria).
About A.D. 200.—The impressive
colonnade, nearly a mile long, was the
main thoroughfare of the city. Also a
sacred way, it comprised a 36 foot
wide central avenue open to the sky,
flanked by covered walks
each 20 feet in width.
George Rodger, Magnum.

Deir el Bari.
Funerary temple
of Queen Hatshepsut.
15th century B. C.
Michel Audrain.

We never say more about ourselves than in the ways we fashion our gods and the temples we build to house them. The Egyptians' determination to hold to the certainties of a limited and self-contained universe, protected by every regulation that law and religion could devise against decay and intrusion, produced finally the temple carved back into the solid rock of cliffs. It is a tribute to human ingenuity and a comment on the range of religious experience that medieval architects could take the same material, stone, to build the cathedrals and deny the ideas the Egyptians confirmed, discarding the world as a fetter instead of holding to it as a refuge.

58

Egyptian. Osiris, god of the netherworld and of the hereafter. Late Period. Brooklyn Museum.

Art and the gods

Greek temples tell us of the Greek adoration of sensuous beauty controlled by a cooler passion for logic. Roman ones, like Roman buildings in general, are triumphantly grandiose, glorifying pride of power. The gods and goddesses carved to inhabit these temples were created by man in his own image and perfected to summarize his own attributes, intellectual, moral and passionate, at ideal levels. The classical gods are the refined and sophisticated descendants, many generations removed, of the sinister or benign spirits imagined by primitive men who, being in a more precarious relationship to nature, had even more reason to court the supernatural.

In Greece and Rome, the distinction between the earthly and the divine was more one of degree than of kind. If the gods were supermen, so could a hero be nearly a god. But religions developed in which there were no supermen gods, but a single God supreme in His all-powerful love and wrath. To give Him material existence through the hands of mortals subject to His highest law seemed audacity, so statues of gods became idols, and Jehovah told Moses, "Thou shalt not make unto thee a graven image, nor any likeness of anything that is in heaven above, or that is in the water under the earth; thou shalt not bow down thyself unto them, nor serve them..." The Jews held to this commandment, and the Moslems to a similar restriction. In India, before the conquest of Alexander, Buddha could not be represented except by his throne, his parasol, and the traces of his steps.

But such restrictions are difficult to observe. Men yearn for the comfort and assurance of a tangible proxy between themselves and their gods. Christianity, after much self-questioning, yielded to this yearning, first with the hieratic, unreal images of the Byzantine icon, and finally with full-fledged realism in which the Virgin and Child, the Christ, and even God the Father were represented in painting and sculpture as tangible beings compassionately assuring men that divine power is tempered by divine mercy and an understanding of human frailty. Temples and cathedrals may be the supreme expressions of our aspirations, but the images of our gods are the most intimate revelations of our needs. Gods appear in varying forms less because men differ at heart than because they search in so many directions.

Art and the gods

Mayan. Detail of the Temple
of the Jaguars at Chichen Itza.
Roger Viollet.

Mayan. The "Castillo" of Chichen
Itza in Yucatan (Mexico).
10th-11th centuries.—This pyramid
with a temple at the summit is at the
site of what was a gory sacrificial
cult. The Maya propitiated their
gods with human blood. *Roger Viollet.*

Toltec. Cinteotl.
Corn god. Limestone.
Museo Nacional, Mexico.
Gisèle Freund.

Temple of Heaven at Peking. Built in 1420
in the Ming Dynasty, it is situated at the
center of a vast gardened quadrilateral
space and rests on a triple platform of white
marble. The temple itself has three
gold-walled tiers separated by roofs of
colored tile. A sacrificial ceremony
took place here every year at
the winter solstice. *Marc Ribaud, Magnum.*

Chinese. Bodhisattva.
Wei Dynasty, beginning of the
6th century. Metropolitan
Museum, New York.
Museum photograph.

Byzantine. Church of the monastery at
Gratchanitsa (southern Yugoslavia) built in 1321
on the "Field of Blackbirds" by order
of Urosh II Milutin.—Although of late
construction and modest scale, it adheres faithfully
to the Byzantine basilica scheme dictated by a
rigid symbolism: a cubic mass representing the
tangible world topped by a dome suggesting the
vault of heaven. *Mladen Grcevic, Zagreb.*

Byzantine. Andrei Rublëv. The Trinity. Icon. 1411. Tretyakov Gallery, Moscow.

The life of the grave

The grave is a fact of life, and no matter how convinced a man is that he will enter paradise, he feels the need for some transition between this world and the next, and the idea of earthly oblivion is abhorrent to him. The abruptness of his departure must be softened, and his entrance into the unknown facilitated. And so we have always marked our graves, whether with a pair of crossed sticks to ward off evil spirits, or with a stone lettered with a name, two dates, and a reassuring inscription. More elaborately we have furnished our tombs with effigies of the things we have most enjoyed, and have pictured ourselves in prayer or offering gifts to the gods we believe in, something in the way we carry letters of introduction when we start a long trip.

Thus death becomes a source of art, but the paradox of funerary art is that it can be created only by the living. It can bring us only to the edge of whatever has already been revealed to the commemorated dead. It can be the most silent art of all, answering questions only by their echo.

But overwhelmingly, funerary art tells us more of the joy of life, and its dignity, than of the horror of death. And when it tells of death, the terms are not of doubt but of certitude. Philippe Pot on his tomb with his dog at his feet is serene and confident. The Etruscan husbands and wives atop their sarcophagi are happily alive, not fearing an end of their mutual bliss but

Burgundian. Antoine Le Moiturier. Tomb of Philippe Pot, "grand sénéchal de Bourgogne," who died in 1493. Louvre, Paris.—Philippe Pot himself saw to the making of his tomb which was originally in the family chapel in a Cistercian monastery.

Etruscan. Sarcophagus from Caere (Cerveteria), a sovereign city of Etruria. Painted terra cotta. 6th century B.C. Louvre, Paris.—The alert-looking couple, reclining on a couch in a life-like pose, once held bowls of fruit or cakes in their hands as offerings. *André Vigneau.*

serene in the confidence of its perpetuation. The thousands of figures from Egyptian and Chinese tombs are forever unquenchably alive.

Individuals may not have felt about their own deaths in the way the art of tombs tells us that they felt, but art in the long run is not concerned with individuals even though it does originate with them. In his contemplation of death, the artist has often dealt with its anguish. But in funerary art he comfortingly regards it not as an isolated and terrible phenomenon opposed to life, but as a point in life that affords a perspective on the best of it. Sometimes a lament that all men must die, funerary art is more often a celebration of the ways in which they have lived.

67

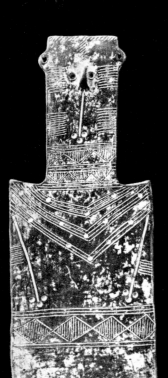

1—Thracian. Horseman. Votive marble relief. Louvre, Paris. *Archives photographiques.*

2—Roman. Votive hand dedicated to the Jupiter Heliopolitanus of Baalbek (Lebanon). Bronze, once gilded. Louvre, Paris.

3—Cycladic. The Zither Player of Keros. Marble idol. 2500-2000 B.C. National Museum, Athens. *Louis Frédéric.*

4—Japanese. Terra-cotta figurine. Jomon period. 1st millennium B.C. Musée Guimet, Paris. *Giraudon.*

5—Cypriote. Probably a fertility goddess. Polished terra cotta. 3rd millennium B.C. Louvre, Paris. *Archives photographiques.*

6—Greek. Figurine from Tanagra. Late 4th to 2nd Centuries B.C. Louvre, Paris. *Giraudon.*

7—Chinese. Dancer. Funerary figurine. Han Dynasty. 206 B.C.-A.D. 220. Musée Cernuschi, Paris. *Giraudon.*

8—Babylonian. Man praying. Found at Larsa. Bronze and gold. Beginning of the 2nd millennium B.C. Louvre, Paris.

3

7

8

Heroes

Gods are inherited from century to century, and the forms they were first given may grow empty. But each generation chooses its own heroes. The hero is a temporal god, and as the object of applause he is a spontaneous indication of the ideals of his time.

In art, the hero shares the eminence of the gods, and it was natural that he should first be sculptured in Greece, where the gods themselves were shown as perfect human beings. The victorious athlete in the Olympic games was not only admired for his prowess, but could also be a symbol of the complete man. The Charioteer of Delphi is brother to another charioteer, Apollo.

There was no beauty of person to celebrate in Balzac, and no reason, either, why his particular body or particular head should make an appropriate symbol of his mind. Rodin's Balzac is not really a portrait and is more than a tribute to one hero-writer. It is a craggy monument to the exploring intellect of the 19th century.

Heroes in art often appear in disguise. Donatello apotheosized the early Renaissance hero as a questing youth, aware of an opening world and alert in his anticipation of conquering it. He could, of course, have been shown as a princely brigand. Donatello showed him as St. George.

Greek. The Charioteer of Delphi. Bronze. About 470 B.C. Delphi Museum.

French. Rodin. Statue of Balzac. Next to last version. 1896. Musée Rodin, Paris.

Italian. Donatello. Saint George, patron saint of the guild of arms makers. 1416. Museo Nazionale (Bargello), Florence.

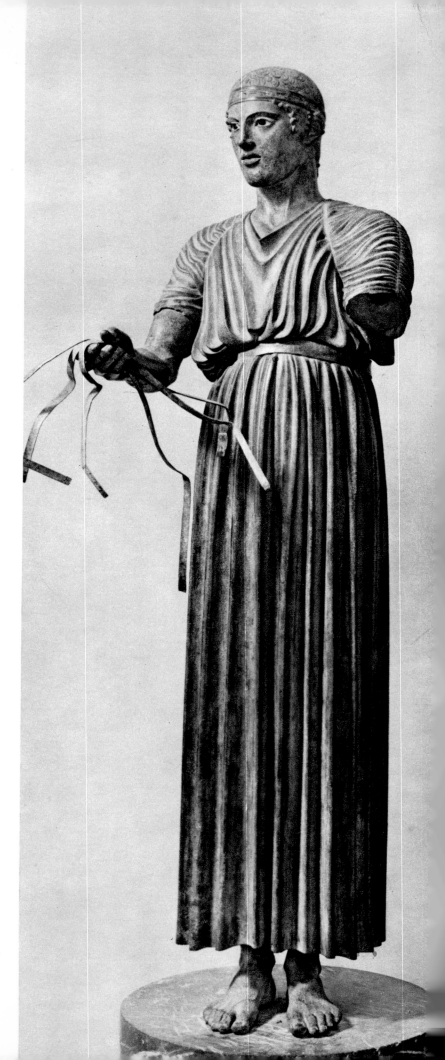

Italian. Titian. The Emperor Charles V. 1548.
Alte Pinakothek, Munich. Titian who, since 1533 had been official portraitist to the Emperor, was summoned to Augsburg in 1548 to paint a royal portrait once again. Charles V, surrounded by a brilliant court of princes and prelates, was then at the zenith of his power.

Like other people, painters and sculptors require food and shelter, but today they go about finding them in an oddly reversed manner. The sensible person recognizes, as a prerequisite condition of life, the operation of a system that creates demands, whether for good typewriting or for the skillful management of money in large quantities, and he adjusts to circumstances by becoming either a stenographer or a banker. But painters and sculptors are not sensible people. They create something we do not seem to need, or at least do not know we need and do not demand. The artist creates not because anyone asks him to create, but for his own satisfaction, and then hopes that he may be able to live by selling something that people have not asked for.

This relationship to the society in which he lives is a complete reversal of the artist's original position. In his earliest form he must have been a member of the tribe who, like the hunter, was delegated the portion of tribal activity for which he was best suited. In a more complex society he became a skilled craftsman, sometimes anonymous, sometimes famous, who supplied a product for which there was a natural demand. Statues were wanted for buildings, so there were sculptors for much the same kind of reason that there were stonemasons. Pictures were demanded as decorations, records, or for votive purposes, so there were painters to supply them, much as there were weavers to supply cloth because cloth was needed.

But in any society the artist is concerned with things of the spirit, and hence artists grew more and more to be recognized as exceptional people. It may be that even the tribal artists of prehistoric times shared some of the prestige of the magic-making priest. Between the two poles of the artist as an unassuming craftsman and the artist as we know him today—an independent esthetic

German. Lucas Cranach. The Electors of Saxony: Frederick the Wise, John the Constant, John Frederick the Magnanimous. Kunsthalle, Hamburg. Cranach's activities at the court of Saxony, to which Frederick the Wise appointed him painter in 1505, are documented almost year by year. His commissions included altarpieces, secular paintings, decorations for the Elector's hunting lodges, works for other princes as well, and were of a number that necessitated his hiring many assistants.

Flemish. Van Dyck.
Charles I of England. 1635.
Louvre, Paris.
This is undoubtedly
the best portrait that Van Dyck
has left us of his royal friend.
White satin jacket, red trousers,
wide-brimmed black hat and fawn
boots contrast effectively and
suggest a life of elegance,
luxury, refinement and leisure.
Giraudon.

Spanish. Velasquez. The Infanta
Maria Theresa. About 1651.
Louvre, Paris.—Hoping to find a
royal suitor for his young daughter,
Philip IV, King of Spain,
commissioned Velasquez to paint two
portraits of her which he sent as
ambassadors in effect, one to
the court of Vienna, the other to
Versailles. The second of the two,
the one shown here, was successful;
in 1660 Maria Theresa was given
in marriage to Louis XIV.

dictator—there was a golden age when the artist had to be a supreme craftsman to supply an ardently demanded product but was also respected for his creative genius. This was the period of the great commissions, when the Church, the State, and the powerful individual desirous of glorifying a religion, a dynasty, or himself, selected the artist most skillful at fulfilling the conditions and accepted him as an equal. It was a time when artists could be courted by Popes or princes, when a Titian, a Raphael, a Van Dyck or a Rubens might live on a truly princely scale, when an entire city might give itself over to parades and festivities to celebrate the completion of an altarpiece for the cathedral, and when Michelangelo during his lifetime could be awarded the epithet "the divine." It was a time when consummate craftsmanship served consummate expression—the time we think of when we say "the old masters."

Duomo, Siena.
12th-15th centuries.

In 1308 the city of Siena commissioned the painter Duccio di Buoninsegna to execute an altarpiece for the cathedral showing the Madonna in majesty surrounded by adoring saints, with various small panels on the reverse of the large one, and surrounding it, to tell the stories of the life of the Virgin and the Passion of her Son.

Three years later the altarpiece, with its dozens of panels set into a golden structure that rose into spires and pinnacles like a miniature edifice, was carried in triumph from the artist's studio just outside the city to the cathedral. The procession wound through the streets and around the public square preceded by trumpeters and other musicians, attended by clerical and city dignitaries carrying candles, and followed by the citizens, who had closed their shops and given over the day to the festival.

Siena was a small, proud city that cherished its aristocratic tradition against the assaults, both intellectual and military, of its burgeoning neighbor, Florence. Like many other cities it dedicated itself to the Virgin, but Siena felt that it had the legitimate claim to her patronage. The altarpiece showed her in truly regal majesty, at once tender and aloof, not only the Queen of Heaven but the Queen of Siena. In picturing her and in the narrative panels Duccio perfected a traditional style appropriate to Siena, a style that insisted on the observance of convention and the importance of elegance, yet was brilliant with poetic life and firm in its statement of faith.

This masterpiece is now sadly dismembered. In 1771 it was divided into

National Gallery, Washington.

National Gallery, Washington.

Museo dell'Opera del Duomo, Siena.

Panels from the back
of the Maestà.

Italian. Duccio di Buoninsegna. Maestà (Madonna in Majesty). 1308-1311. Museo dell'Opera del Duomo, Siena.—Originally an altarpiece painted front and back, the front (above) showed the Madonna Enthroned with saints and angels; the back was 53 panels with scenes from the life of Christ. The two faces, separated, have been exhibited thus since 1795. Some panels are dispersed, a few are lost.

its separate panels, some of which are lost; some others are in collections around the world. In its violated state the greatest Sienese painting is now housed in a museum adjacent to the cathedral, but we still have the record of an anonymous chronicler who saw the procession and reminds us that on June 9, 1311, the bells of Siena "sounded the Gloria in homage to so noble a painting as this."

National Gallery, London.
Museo del Opera del Duomo, Siena.
National Gallery, Washington.

Left wing of the triptych: Saint Anthony and
Saint Thomas with Tommaso Portinari and his two sons.
Anderson-Giraudon.

Flemish. Hugo van der Goes. The Adoration of the Shepherds.

Donations to temples and religious institutions had been
common in all ages but this sort of gift took on a special
character in the Middle Ages and the Renaissance with
the rise of mercantile cities and republics. There was an
exceptional interest in painting and it became a custom for
the rich bourgeoisie to offer paintings to their churches as
tokens of zeal and piety. Wanting to be identified with
their donations, they had themselves included as participants in the pictured events. In the beginning they were
content to appear as bystanders, inconspicuous in groups

Central panel of the Portinari Altarpiece. 1476-1478. Uffizi, Florence.

Right wing of the triptych. Saint Margaret and Saint Mary Magdalene with Maria Portinari and her daughter.
Anderson-Giraudon.

of witnesses to the legend of their choice. They soon demanded to be set apart, accompanied only by their patron saints as intercessors. Of the masterpieces that followed what became a convention, the Portinari altarpiece is perhaps the most famous. Commissioned in 1476 by Tommaso Portinari, representative in the Netherlands for the bank of the Medici, it was painted by Hugo van der Goes in Bruges and, on completion, transported to Florence for installation on the high altar of the Medici family chapel in the church of Sant'Egidio.

77

Dutch. Rembrandt. Syndics of the Amsterdam
Cloth Guild. 1662. Rijksmuseum, Amsterdam.
Painted for the drapers' guildhall,
this was one of the last commissions
accepted by the artist. He had delivered the
famous "Night Watch" twenty years earlier,
in 1642, to the guild of arms makers
and had painted the "Lesson in Anatomy
by Professor Deyman" for the society of
surgeons in 1656.
Museum photograph.

German. These two statues stand in an
impressive row of twelve, ranged
against the pillars of the choir
in the cathedral of Naumburg in Saxony.
Carved in 1255 and 1265, they
commemorate the founders of the
church. The two here are Prince
Ekkehardt and Princess Uta
Bildarchiv Foto Marburg.

Spanish. El Greco. The Burial of the Count of Orgaz. 1586. Santo Tomé, Toledo.—This
monumental masterpiece is the perfect example of a commissioned work. The subject
was assigned: to tell the story of a miraculous happening at the church of Santo Tomé in
the course of a funeral service for the nobleman, Gonzalo Ruiz of Toledo, Count of Orgaz.
A legend persisted that Saint Augustine and Saint Stephen appeared and took part in the
burial themselves as reward to the Count for his piety. He had left the church a legacy
but the city, which was to administer it, defaulted on its payment. More than two centuries
later, in 1586, Santo Tomé's parish priest took up the matter of this old debt, sued the city
and won his suit. As homage to the benefactor of his church he asked El Greco to paint
a retelling of the miracle. The contract drawn up not only settled the price for the work
(1200 ducats) but described the required composition in minutest detail: "A procession must
be painted showing exactly how the priest and his assistants conducted the Mass and how
the two saints descended to bury the nobleman's body, how one held his head and the other
his feet, how they placed him in his tomb. Many people must be standing around and,
overhead, the sky must open on Paradise." El Greco made portraits of contemporaries to
stand in for the nobles, priests and monks taking part in or watching the ceremony. He even
included the Santo Tomé priest, Andrès Nuñez, and dressed him in the surplice he wanted
to be shown wearing.
Anderson-Giraudon.

Flemish. Petrus Christus.
Saint Eloy. 1449. Robert Lehman
Collection, New York.
This painting of Saint Eloy as a
goldsmith showing a ring to an engaged
couple was made on order from the
goldsmith's guild of Antwerp, a valued
commission to judge by the prominence
given certain objects and the
meticulousness with which they are
painted: the fabrics, for instance,
jewels, gleaming vessels,
the gold-framed mirror. We are told
not only how well-off people were
in the mid-15th century but also
how much influence the prosperous
business world was beginning
to impose on art.
Giraudon.

Any important work of architecture
was of necessity commissioned into existence
A contemporary commission resulted in this
building in Paris, the seat of UNESCO
and the collaboration of three internationally
known architects: Marcel Breuer (U.S.A.), Pier
Nervi (Italy), Bernard Zehrfuss (France).
In the foreground is a sculpture
by Henry Moore (England) created for the
entrance esplanade. 1957-1958.
Pierre Belzeaux, Rapho.

Paolo Uccello. First panel of the
"Battle of San Romano." 1456.
Louvre, Paris.
Laboratoire du Musée.

These three panels were ordered for a celebration in 1456 honoring Niccoló da Tolentino, a hero who, as general, had led the Florentines to victory over the Sienese at the battle of San Romano in 1432.

Paolo Uccello. Final panel of the
"Battle of San Romano." 1456.
National Gallery, London. *Giraudon.*

Italian. Simone Martini. Equestrian portrait
of Guidoriccio dei Fogliani da Reggio. 1328.
Palazzo Pubblico, Siena.—This fresco
commemorates the victory won at Maremma
in 1328 by Guidoriccio, Sienese general,
riding triumphant here between the two
strongholds, Montemassi and Sassoforte, which
he captured. Symbol of the chivalrous and
martial spirit of the Republic of Siena,
the hero is in parade dress astride his white
horse, which was killed in the Montemassi assault.
Arborio Mella, Milan.

Italian. Paolo Uccello. Central panel of the "Battle of San Romano." 1456. Uffizi, Florence.

Italian. Verrocchio.
Bartolommeo Colleoni. 1483-1488. Campo
dei Santi Giovanni e Paolo, Venice.
The Republic of Venice erected this
forceful **monument** to the "condottieri,"
the mercenary army commander who had
willed it a sizeable fortune.
Anderson-Giraudon.

Flemish. David Teniers the Younger. The gallery of the Archduke Leopold-Wilhelm in Brussels. About 1652. Prado, Madrid.—This picture tells in extraordinary detail about a great collection of painting. Archduke Leopold-Wilhelm, brother of the Austrian Emperor, Ferdinand III, was appointed governor of the Spanish Netherlands in 1646. He had spent years at the Spanish court in Madrid, had come to know the treasures in the collections of Charles V and Philip II, had developed a serious interest in and love for painting and had progressed so far with a collection of his own that he had 517 paintings by Italian masters to bring with him when he took up his post in Brussels. In 1647 he appointed David Teniers the Younger his court painter and curator. Teniers was of invaluable help to him both in arranging and maintaining the works already acquired and in advising him about purchases of new ones, particularly when they were by Dutch or Flemish artists. When Leopold-Wilhelm retired from the governorship ten years later, he had 1,397 paintings to take with him to Vienna. He willed them "as my most noble and favorite possession" to his nephew, the Emperor Leopold I; they eventually became the main portion of the Kunsthistorisches Museum. In this Vienna museum now is another of the several records of the gallery that Teniers painted from different points of view. In the one above Leopold-Wilhelm is coming toward us from the right; to the left is the Count of Fuensaldana, a rich fellow-collector, and, behind the table, is the artist himself. *Giraudon.*

Shown here in the Gallery are three Titians:
   left, "Nymph and Shepherd;" center, "Diana and Callisto" and, on the right, "Danae;" the "Portrait of a Woman" is Palma Vecchio's and the "Doge Niccoló da Ponte" is by Tintoretto;
on the left-hand wall, three down and taking up the whole space is a canvas by Veronese, "Christ Healing the Woman with the Issue of Blood;" below it, Titian's "Jesus and the Woman Taken in Adultery;"
on the right-hand wall, second row, the "Adoration of the Magi" by Veronese and a "Descent from the Cross" by Tintoretto; in the fourth, a famous Giorgione called "The Three Philosophers" (partly hidden).
Standing on the floor in the foreground:
to the left, Gossart's "Saint Luke Painting the Virgin" and next to it, "Saint Sebastian" by Veronese;
to the right, with drapery across one corner, "Saint Margaret Slaying the Dragon" by Giulio Romano; on smaller canvasses, the "Portrait of a Woman at her Toilette" by Titian, "Violante" by Palma Vecchio (sometimes attributed to Titian), "The Archduchess Isabelle, Regent of the Low Countries, Dressed as a Carmelite" by Rubens; also by Rubens, the large black-framed picture, "The Circumcision".

The new maecenas

From the caves of prehistory to the glossy art salesrooms of today is a long journey that the artist has traveled over a course determined by the changing character of the times. A major turning came near the end of the seventeenth century. Until then the artist worked largely for the church or for the great princes, but after 1600 a new class began to show strength, a class that was to change the nature of art. This middle class had already hinted at its power with the wealthy financier upon whom a king might have to depend; it flourished in the persons of the prosperous burghers whose banking and trading became the warp and woof of the fabric of society.

The wealthy bourgeois loved to buy and own things. The acquisition of curious and expensive objects was a tribute to his intellect and his purse. In his comfortable house he liked to have pictures of his comfortable self and his comfortable wife, of scenes and things that were familiar. Art began to treat of less grandiose themes, on a less grandiose scale. This could have meant vulgarization in an unhappy sense of the word, and it did mean that art was subjected to a powerful widening process, which frequently must involve a lowering one as well. But within the new bourgeois class there developed the connoisseur-collector and the collector-patron, the man of taste and intellect who not only gathered about himself whatever he could buy of the art of the past, making of himself a sort of prince by purchase, but who was interested in discovering the painters of the day who deserved and needed his support. The eighteenth century produced the prototype of the nineteenth and twentieth century collectors for whom, increasingly, the satisfactions of discovery and patronage are at least equal to the esthetic enjoyment of the discovered art.

As the bourgeoisie increased in numbers and became increasingly eager to share in the cultivation of the arts, middlemen became necessary to perform functions that had been unnecessary in a society where a relatively small number of patrons could deal directly with a relatively small number of artists. Finally art became merchandise; the rule became not the commission executed on specific order, but the picture painted and then offered for sale. As esthetic brokers, the Salon and the critic joined the dealer. Most recently, museums of modern art have combined the functions of all three.

French. Matisse.
Doctor Claribel Cone. 1933.
The Cone sisters, Claribel and Etta, are rightly called pioneers among American collectors of modern art. They bought canvasses by Picasso and Matisse as long ago as 1905 and their enthusiasm for Matisse never diminished. There are 43 of his paintings, 18 of his sculptures and 113 drawings by him in their legacy to the Baltimore Museum of Art

French. Cézanne.
Victor Chocquet. 1877.
Gallery of Fine Arts, Columbus, Ohio.—A modes customs clerk, Chocquet had an unbounded admiration for the impressionists before they were recognized and generally known. Renoir, who also painted a portrait of him, and Cézanne, whom he met in 1875, were both close friends. At his death, Chocquet's enviable collection included 11 Renoirs, 32 Cézannes.

French. Géricault. Signboard for a blacksmith. 1819.
Private collection, Paris.

French. Watteau. Signboard of Gersaint. 1720.
Charlottenburg Palace, Berlin.—Wanting to repay
Gersaint for hospitality, the artist dashed off this
painting in a few days and sent it to the dealer
to use as a signboard for his shop at 35 Pont-Notre Dame.
The persons represented are members of Gersaint's family,
employees and regular clients. The portrait of
Louis XIV being put into a crate in the left foreground
is an allusion to the name of the shop which was
"Au grand Monarque." *Archiv für Kunst.*

The new maecenas

The trouble with the official exhibition, the dealer,
and the critic as middlemen between artist and public
is that they cannot limit themselves to pointing out and
gathering together what is available. They decide
what should be made available on the basis of quality
as they see it, and thus become tastemakers. During
the latter nineteenth century the system all but strangled
some of the artists whom we now recognize as the great
ones of a great age in painting. They were saved by
occasional dealers like Durand-Ruel and Ambroise Vol-
lard, an occasional critic like Zola, and by a handful of
perceptive collectors. The lesson has made us wary but
the tastemaker's position is always a shaky one. One
thing is certain, however: in a democratic and commercial
age, the dealer catering to the collector has replaced
the church and the state as art's sustaining patron.

The artist witness of his time

We tend to have the idea, exaggerated by the removed position into which art has been forced today, that the artist is a man outside the usual conventions and obligations of society. Often he assumes this position of his own accord, happily seizing advantages offered by the concept of a creative person as a free spirit whose imaginative power may be cramped or thwarted by such observances of convention as getting a haircut at regular intervals, keeping appointments, and conforming in general to the hundreds of practical obligations that rule the rest of us, whether we like them or not, from the cradle where our parents begin to enforce the pattern to the grave where we are finally lowered according to the health laws of the community and the ritual of our faith.

The artist-as-rebel may be doing nothing more than indulging in a pose convenient for him but irritating to everyone else. Yet even this pose had a legitimate origin in the nineteenth century when the artist-as-bohemian was born in protest against a bourgeois society in which conformity to a peculiarly unimaginative standard was elevated to the status of a social religion. Faced with a social dictum that said, in effect, "Conform or die," the artist responded with a counter-dictum, "To conform is to die," and then hunted for the fullest life in ways that seemed odd to most people.

One may wonder, today, why so many artists who appear to have so little connection with life in their work, whose work seems so entirely a studio product divorced from the problems of concern to the rest of us, are found marching in protest parades, joining picket lines, writing letters of indignation to the papers when they think they have found instances of stupidity, injustice or cruelty, and allying themselves with political movements promising revolution or reform. These artists are only following, outside the studio, a tradition that has a noble, if limited, tradition within the studio—the tradition of the artist as a witness of his times who is stirred to anger by individuals or systems that debase the human spirit, to compassion for those human beings whose spiritual nobility persists in the face of violation, and to fervor for those revolutions in which men have risen against their oppressors.

This kind of social statement in art appeared late. For centuries the artist reflected the ideal of a society and passed its imperfections by. This was to

The artist witness of his time

be expected when art was commissioned by the ruling princes or the established church—or was not commissioned at all, and hence not produced. The artist as prosecutor was a rare phenomenon ; one finds only occasional isolated instances, such as Botticelli lamenting (in allegory) the execution of Savonarola, and Bruegel recording (in disguise) the Spanish persecution of Flanders.

But with the seventeenth century the artist began a course in social consciousness. Louis Le Nain's picture of a peasant family on the opposite page is anything but a picture of protest, but it is important as an early recognition that dignity exists even in the substrata of society. Above all else this is a beautiful painting, beautiful in the serenity of its arrangement, in the perfection of its drawing, in its fall of light. But the exceptional element is that these purely esthetic delights, equally delightful when employed in a portrait of a prince and his family, are used expressively to invest a family of peasants with a dignity even more impressive than princely dignity because it is warmer, deeper, a part of all human life.

At about the same time, in Spain, Murillo discovered beggars and ragamuffins in a comparable way—but the comparison is not to Murillo's advantage. Unlike Le Nain's self-contained peasants, who inspire our respect, Murillo's beggar boy asks for our pity, or at least Murillo makes him do so. This is sentimentality, by which our act of conceding pity reflects to our own credit first. Le Nain leads us to admire his noble peasants ; Murillo allows us to admire our own specious nobility. Yet, slight and diluted though it may be, Murillo's element of sympathy for a boy who heretofore would have been painted only as a bit of picturesque detail is a symptom of something stirring in the consciousness of a painter who worked in the context of a corrupt, flaccid and stagnating nation.

Sentimentality and bombast are the twin dangers of painting as partisan social statement ; the artist who escapes them is the artist who may be partisan, but who is stirred less as a partisan than as a person by the spectacle of the world's evils. Thus Diego Rivera, a violent partisan politically, could do a "Liberation of the Peon" which was less a political statement of Mexico's agrarian revolution than a hymn to the strong who succor the weak. Goya showing

French. Louis Le Nain. Peasant Family in an Interior.
About 1643. Louvre, Paris. *Giraudon.*

The three Le Nains, who came from
Vermandois, worked together.
They are known for the dignity
and verisimilitude of their treatment
of 17th century peasant life.

Spanish. Murillo. Young Beggar
Delousing Himself. 1645-1655.
Louvre, Paris.—Murillo had more
commissions than he could accept
but he escaped from them, now and
then all his life, to indulge his
interest in common people: happy
children, beggars, dice players,
flower sellers, gypsies. He gave
them the everyday but picturesque
background of the Spain he
knew. *Bulloz.*

Mexican. Diego Rivera. **The Liberation of the Peon. 1931.** Philadelphia Museum of Art.—Rivera, a revolutionary, felt an obligation to pain his idea of his country's political and social history. He gave modern art a strong push in the direction of social consciousness with his frescos in the Mexican Ministry of Education.

Flemish. Bruegel. The Massacre of the Innocents. 1567. Kunsthistorisches Museum, Vienna.—Occupied by troops of Philip II, the Catholic King of Spain, the Netherlands was in economic disorder, rent by religious conflict, poverty stricken. A "Beggars' Insurrection," led by William the Taciturn, resulted in 1565. The consequent Spanish repression wiped out town after town. Bruegel implicitly expounds the Reformation sweeping the northern countries: he records a searching party of the Inquisition savagely seizing victims in a Flemish town but disguises the episode as a Biblical story.

French. Géricault. Raft of the Medusa. Study. 1818. Louvre, Paris. This painted account of a disaster was inspired by the shipwreck in 1816 of the frigate "Méduse," an event which had scandalous repercussions including impassioned criticism of the ministry accused of putting an incompetent officer in command. In 1817 two of the saved men, the doctor, Savigny, and the engineer, Corréard, published their version of what had happened. The government banned its sale and prosecuted Corréard who had done the printing. In sympathy and outrage, Géricault undertook in an individual way to plead for justice. He got in touch with the two men, had the rescued ship's carpenter build a replica of the Medusa's raft, sought out other survivors and made sketches of them. As models for those who had not survived he used dead and dying patients in the Beaujon hospital. *Giraudon.*

Spanish citizens executed by Napoleonic soldiers on May 3, 1808, and Daumier
showing the bodies of citizens murdered by the government of Louis-Philippe
during the Republican Revolt of 1834, are commenting with bitterness and fury
upon specifically identifiable instances of inhumanity, but the power of these
pictures as art comes from the universal application of their indictments of
man's inhumanity to man, all specific references aside. And although Delacroix's "Liberty Leading the People" is a tribute to the uprising of July 28, 1830,
it is even more a statement of the will to justice that is still the hope of the world.

Spanish. Goya. The Executions of May 3, 1808. Prado, Madrid.—In the spring of 1814 the Regency asked Goya to "immortalize with the brush the glorious uprising of Spain against the Tyrant of Europe." He did so, in his own way, choosing to commemorate in two paintings the second and third days of May 1808 when a revolt of Madrid's ragged, unarmed populace was brutally crushed by Napoleonic troops. *Anderson-Viollet.*

French. Delacroix. Scenes of the Massacres of Scio. 1824. Louvre, Paris.—Since 1821 all Europe had been watching the Greeks struggle to regain independence. Byron joined them in beseiged Missolonghi and died there in 1824. Hugo was writing and publishing the most flaming of his "Orientales." Entered in the Salon of 1824 this painting had at this exactly right time its greatest possible effect. Inspired by accounts of a Turkish massacre on the island of Scio in 1822 it dramatized the martyrdom of the 30,000 Greeks who were killed there or taken as slaves. *Giraudon.*

French. Daumier, **Rue Transnonain.** 1834. Published soon after the event, this lithograph records the murders perpetrated by the civil guard charged by Louis Philippe with putting down a republican revolt in April 1834. The government had effectively won the day, the republican adherents were subdued, when soldiers, on the pretext of a shot having been fired from windows of this apartment house, burst in and butchered everyone living there. *Roger Viollet.*

French. Delacroix.
Liberty Leading the People. 1830.
Louvre, Paris.—Powder fumes had
scarcely dissipated and paving blocks
been put back into place before
Delacroix started work on this
grandiloquent picture, one of the
most famous to be directly inspired
by a political event. Delacroix was
not a republican but he loved liberty
and, above all, like many of his
contemporaries, had enthusiastically
welcomed the return of the tricolor
during the three historic days
of July 1830.

Accepted by the 1831
Salon and purchased by the State,
the painting was very soon withdrawn
from exhibition at the Luxembourg
for fear that it might encourage
revolt. Aside from a brief
appearance in 1848, it was kept
in the museum's storerooms and the
public did not see it again until
it was shown at the Exposition
Universelle of 1855.

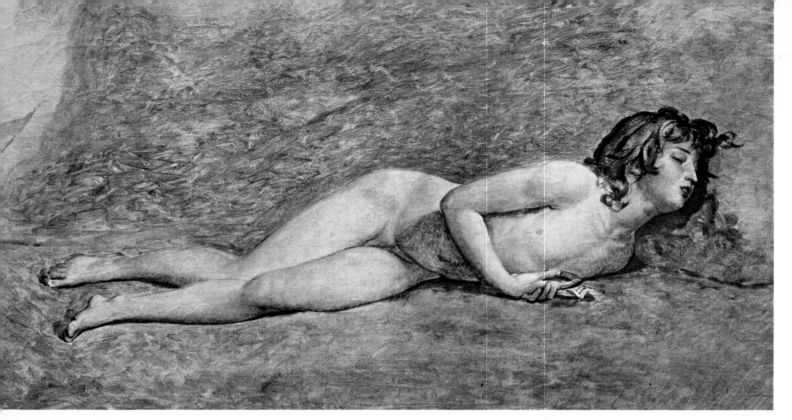

French. Jacques Louis David.
The Death of Bara. 1794.
Musée Calvet, Avignon.—Joseph Bara
was the 13-year-old drummer boy who
taken prisoner by the Vendéens in
December 1793 and commanded to shout
"Vive le Roi !" refused, choosing
rather to face a rifle squad and
to die with the cry "Vive la République !"
This act of heroism immediately became
legendary and has been celebrated by
writers as well as by painters.
In his "Vie de Napoléon" Stendhal
describes the access of hero worship
aroused in him and his childhood
companions by the story of the little
republican drummer boy. *Bulloz.*

French. Picasso. Guernica. 1937. On loan from
the artist to the Museum of Modern Art, New York.

The artist witness of his time

A painter offering social evidence must **reach** us with the force of an eye-witness. When he fails, he gives us a "Death of Bara," a drama of heroic death reduced to an exercise in drawing the nude. Can we blame an unfortunate combination of subject and style? No; there is the immediate refutation of Picasso's "Guernica." Who would have suspected that these intellectually synthesized forms could suddenly burst into such passionate expression, could produce a painting that reaches us with the immediacy of a scream? After the fact we recognize a fortunate coincidence between the semi-cubist breaking up of form and modern war's technique of mass destruction, but this is virtually a play on words.   The force comes from the artist's conviction, which reaches us through his mastery of whatever style of painting.

The artist as soliloquist

Artists have painted their own portraits for various reasons—least often, probably, from vanity; very often simply as a record, in the manner of other portraits; sometimes because the mirror offers a convenient and willing model as tireless as the painter himself, ready to pose for an exercise in a craft. During the Renaissance, self-portraits might be included among groups of other figures partly in the nature of a signature. Thus Botticelli painted himself among his friends and patrons, the Medici, as an attendant at the Adoration of the Magi; thus Mantegna is among his frescoed Gonzagas and their courtiers who are gathered in the Camera degli Sposi in the family palace in Mantua. And Michelangelo dared paint his own portrait into the Last Judgment in the Sistine Chapel, where his caricatured features hang distorted and agonized as part of the flayed skin of St. Bartholomew, dangling from the hands of his executioner among the damned.

But the self-portrait in its most significant form is much more than the record of a set of features brought into context as part of a larger scheme. In its most thoughtful form the self-portrait occupies a place in painting similar to the soliloquy's in the drama, when the protagonist stands alone and speaks to himself, examining the nature of the world and his own place in it, asking how circumstance has put him into a position that seems to have been arrived at entirely without showing him which next action is inevitably right. In fathoming his own features, the artist becomes his own Hamlet, soliloquizing during the drama of his own life. The soliloquy is not always tragic, since life is not always tragic. We know the young Dürer from his delineations of a handsome, determined man charged with the pride and energy of youth; Rubens' mirror showed him a big, glowing, confident man whose full-blooded physical experience was amplified by an intelligence adaptable to brilliant worldly success. The range of self-portraits is as wide as the range of character in men who have become artists, as wide as the range of experience life has allowed them, and as deep as their power to relay to the rest of us whatever wisdom this experience brings them. In this power, in these soliloquies, one name stands above all others: Rembrandt.

Full page: Dutch. Rembrandt
Self-portrait. 1659. Mellon Collection
National Gallery, Washington

Gauguin. 1890.

Van Dyck. 1621-1622.

Goya. About 1793.

Picasso. 1906.

Matisse. 1937.

Dürer. 150

By the objective standard of straight physical record, a gallery of Rembrandt's self-portraits chronologically arranged is a technically brilliant study of the progressive changes in a face from early youth to old age. The record is arresting enough in itself since everyone must be sensitive to its subjective implications. If we correlate our knowledge of Rembrandt's life with the dates of the individual pictures, our response becomes more specialized: this portrait was painted when he was hardly more than a student; this one at the time of his marriage to his beloved Saskia in 1634, when his professional success was bolstered by a social one; this one during the heyday of his public career and his private happiness; this one at the time of Saskia's death in 1642 and the unexpected failure of an important commission, a sudden change in his fortunes; this one at the time of his bankruptcy in 1656, when he lost his fine house and his splendid collection; and so on, until the end of a life that began with fame and fortune and ended in relative obscurity and impoverishment.

But this makes too much of the factual history of Rembrandt's life and too little of the history that really counted. His change of worldly status was only partially the result of misfortunes. His withdrawal from the high, wide and handsome scene of his younger days was at least as much the result of deepening personal philosophy as it was of evil circumstance. It is true that his self-portraits show an increasingly battered face, but they also show increasingly the dignity of the human spirit triumphant in its contemplation of the human condition. The contemplation is often somber, but never bitter, sometimes tragic, but never pathetic, for tragedy is based on the concept of man as noble while pathos implies a smallness, a frailty, a vulnerability, that Rembrandt refused to acknowledge at the core of human experience.

Although Rembrandt found nobility in ordinary men, even in the derelicts

Ingres. 1804.   Degas. About 1866.

from the ghetto who served him as models for kings, he certainly did not think that he had found the perfect image of conventional nobility in his own homely, puffed, lined and sagging old face. Nor was he, except in the early portraits, telling us, "This is what Rembrandt looked like." He became his own best model because, like any wise man in maturity, he understood the world through what it had tried to make of him and the way he had withstood or accepted it. All other knowledge, no matter how deep and how moving, comes to us at second hand.

What Rembrandt tells us in his self-portraits, deep and moving as it is, comes to us at second hand, yet where else can we come so close to identity with another being as here? Paradoxically, one reason is that as Rembrandt painted himself growing older, the image is decreasingly personal. The earlier self-portraits display the features and costume of a certain prosperous man who happened to live in Holland in the first half of the 17th century, and the earliest do little more than describe him. But as the face ages, it is progressively less and less attached to time and place, until we are confronted not by a painter named Rembrandt, but by Everyman. The eyes into which we look might almost be our own ; because his soliloquy becomes universal, we are absorbed into the portrait of an artist who painted three hundred years ago.

Van Gogh. 1887.   Van Gogh. 1887.   Van Gogh. 1888.   Van Gogh. 1889.

III

THE HIGH PLACES

the Acropolis

Jerusalem

Mecca

Pagan

Assisi

Megalithic monument at Stonehenge,
England. Probably about 1500 B.C.
This magical circle of great stones
has not yielded its secret but could
have been a temple dedicated to the sun.
Aerofilms Ltd.

Hittite. Teshub,
god of storms and beneficent rain.
Stele found at Tell Ahmar (Syria).
End of the 2nd millennium B.C.
Probably standing originally
on his sacred animal, a bull,
or on a mountain, this weather
god grasps a symbolic bolt of
lightning in one hand and
brandishes in the other an axe,
symbol of thunder.
Giraudon

The high places were the first homes of the gods. Sprites might inhabit trees or lakes, but the most powerful beings lived on the peaks, which, like themselves, were removed but omnipresent, invulnerable and eternal, requiring, in the natural order of things, that men lift their eyes to them. What other places were so advantageous for the hurling of thunderbolts, the dispatching of rain clouds, and the supervision of subjects whose activities must be followed for punishment or reward according to merit? The high place could be benign or threatening, rising like a protection or a benediction when it was not clouded in wrath. Headlands reared themselves above the horizon of the sea in the first greeting to returning mariners. And always the high places were the juncture between earth, where men were bound, and the sky, where the gods could roam when they wished. Where high places did not exist, they had to be raised. The first religious structures of piled stones approximated natural objects; later the ziggurats and the pyramids were built mountains.

The pyramids, unified with the solar system by defining the points of the compass, catch the first light of the sun on their tips before it appears over the rim of the earth, and hold its last light after it has sunk. They are at once demonstrations of man's powers and his gesture of recognition toward powers he cannot altogether control. But if he cannot control them, he makes

A dolmen
near the Mowne Mountains
in Northern Ireland.

Egyptian. Pyramid of King Snofru,
IV Dynasty, at Dashur, south of
Memphis. About 2670 B.C.—Each side
measures 617 feet at the base and
is 295 feet high. A veritable
mountain in the desert, several
miles from the green valley of the
Nile, both a tomb and a temple, the
pyramid links earth to sky and
assured the Pharaoh his every need for
survival in his afterlife.
Michel Audrain-Samivel.

himself worthy of his gods in the monuments he proffers them. In his pride, he has even made himself the ally of gods as well as their subject. No task has been too great for accomplishment in this double role. To realize their

Sumerian. Ziggurat at Choga Zambil near Susa in Elam (now southern Iran).—Built in the 13th century B.C. of bricks made from river mud, this giant tiered tower, over 160 feet high, was crowned by a temple reached by steps, vestiges of which remain today. Largest of the ziggurats was the lofty Tower of Babel, wonder and curiosity of the ancient world, which the Bible credits with a height of more than 980 feet.
Roger Viollet.

Some 8500 feet high, Sri Pada on the island of Ceylon is a sacred mountain to Buddhists who make pilgrimages to it every year. Moslems also consider it sacred, as do Hindus, who call itSiva's Peak. Adam's Peak is the name by which it is best known.
H. Sochurek, Life Magazine.

fortress temples in the Andes, the Incas of Peru moved stones of a size and weight that would strain our machines, and cut and joined them with a precision we could hardly excel with our scientifically perfected tools. They achieved, in the end, an awesome monument to themselves for although the gods were destroyed with the civilization they could not, after all, protect, the monuments remain to stagger us as testimony to their builders.

The high places used to dominate an earth that was vast because it was a disc that dropped off somewhere into the void. Their majesty should be

Mount Sinai. It was on this barren mountain north of the Red Sea that the Lord appeared to Moses and gave him the tablets of the law. The convent of Saint Catherine is at its foot.
Roger Viollet.

diminished now that the earth has become a pellet in a universe of incomprehensible size. Mountains have been chopped, gashed and hollowed out, and could be disintegrated by new weapons. Entire ranges become miniatures when seen from machines the gods never imagined. But it makes little difference. On the high places where temples still stand, men discovered themselves and established a relationship to the universe of the spirit that sustains them as particles in the universe of science.

Machu-Picchu, city built by the Incas on a natural fortress, a mountain top of the Peruvian Andes 2000 feet above the plunging, roaring Urubamba River below, is northwest of Cuzco, which the Incas called the navel of the world. The photograph here is of a sundial used by the High Priest of the Sun; the smaller one, to the left, shows the pinnacle of Huyana Picchu where the Incas built their last refuge. The stairway to it can still be climbed today.
René Burri, Magnum.

Japanese. Hokusai. Storm with Lightning at the Foot of Fujiyama. Color woodblock. Musée Guimet, Paris.—A volcano extinct for 250 years, this is the highest peak in Japan (12,440 feet). It is a pilgrimage site visited every year by thousands of Japanese.

Mount Olympus, home of the gods. It is nearly 9,700 feet high and snow clings to its slopes even in midsummer. The Greeks made this sacred and awe-inspiring crag the throne of Zeus.
Boissonnas.

The sacred rock of the Acropolis seen from the west with the Parthenon as its crown. This "high city" was the fortified seat of government and housed the more important of the public sanctuaries. Citadel of the gods, it was the cultural center of Attica as well.
Louis Frédéric, Rapho.

The Acropolis is sacred to us all. We are absurd if we speak of the death of the gods who were worshipped there: they are still alive wherever beauty and reason are venerated. They were born with the morning of our self-knowledge, which dawned in Greece and was fullest and brightest on the Acropolis. In sparkling light and crystalline air we learned for the first time how to take our own measure and apply it as a module to all things.

The Parthenon was a joyous building, glittering with gold and bright color, dedicated to a goddess but scaled to men, standing firmly upon an earth where joy and dignity were birthrights to be claimed and defended rather than reaching toward a heaven where they were promises. It was a temple to reason, not mysticism; to intellect, rather than faith. Its design was calculated, not inspired, but its perfection was such that we recognize perfection even in the ruin that stands on the Acropolis today. Its gold and bright color are lost, its sculpture has been ravished, it is scarred and broken, but it is noble, buoyant and strong.

As a triumph of regulated proportion, the Parthenon was a symbol of our capacity for wholeness through knowledge and moderation. Because it is in ruins, it may be a symbol of our failure to hold to an ideal which, for that matter, may not have been fully realized even in the Golden Age except in art. But the ideal was formulated, and the Parthenon in ruins is not a ghostly reminder

The Acropolis

of a past that is lost, but a living affirmation that the ideal is still part of our conscience.

Short of pulverizing it you cannot spoil the Acropolis. It is surrounded by the noisy ugliness of modern Athens ; the celebrants in the processions that mount the sacred steps are tourists who carry cameras and candy bars instead of votive torches and garlands ; they are led by professors and guides instead of by priests. Yet nothing defiles or degrades the Acropolis, and nothing really ages it. It does not dream, it lives.

The Parthenon, east façade
Planned after the Persian wars to replace a destroyed temple, the building and its sculptures took the 15 years from 447 to 432 B.C. to complete and was named after the goddess (Athena Parthenos) to whom it was consecrated.
Roger Viollet.

Interior of the Parthenon.
The temple consisted of two
independent halls. The heroic gold
and ivory statue of Athena by Phidias
stood in the cella, seen here.
A smaller hall, to which the name
"parthenon" or "Hall of the Virgins"
is properly applied, was the
depository for treasure belonging to
the goddess and to the State.
Louis Frédéric, Rapho.

The Erechtheum. It was begun
about 421 and completed in 406 B.C.
This view of the sanctuary from the
south shows the caryatids supporting
the roof of the Porch of the Maidens.
Each is seven and a half feet tall.
It has been a Byzantine church and
in 1463 was used by the Turks to house
the harem of the governor of the city.
Roger Viollet.

Temple of Athena Nike or of the
Wingless Victory (a name given their
goddess by the Athenians in the hope
that she would not leave their city).
Finished about 424 B.C., it is
diminutive in size (about 28 1/2 feet
wide at the base and 18 feet high).
It owes its light grace to beautifully
proportioned Ionic columns front
and back and has a famous
sculptured parapet.
Henri Monnier, Rapho.

On the slope below the Erechtheum,
(to the left) an olive tree is planted
on the spot where, according to legend, Athena
caused an olive tree to spring forth.
Henri Monnier, Rapho.

The Erechtheum and the Parthenon seen
from the entrance portico
called the Propylaea.
L. H. Baker, Atlas-Photo.

The Parthenon.
Pericles, who ordered it built, gave Phidias the responsibility of supervising the construction. The architects were Ictinos and Callicrates. The temple measures approximately 100 feet wide at the base and is nearly 230 feet long. The major remaining fragments of the wonderful sculptures are in the British Museum in London. A few are still on the building; others are scattered in European museums. Pedimental sculpture told the story of Athena's birth, of her contest with Poseidon to determine which one of them should be patron deity of the city. Metopes and friezes depicted battle scenes and the famous Panathenaic procession. The Parthenon is the supreme example of Greek classic art.

Used at one time or another as a Byzantine church, a Catholic cathedral and as a mosque, it was blown up in 1687 in a bombardment by the Venetians at war with the Turks, who had made it a storehouse for ammunition.

Careful archeological research and restoration are giving it more and more of its original appearance.
Louis Frédéric, Rapho.

Jerusalem. In the foreground, the old Jewish cemetery with the Valley of Cedron (or of Jehoshaphat); beyond, Jerusalem's wall with the remains of a Moslem cemetery close to its foot; in the background the city in panorama dominated by the dome of the Mosque of Omar.
Roger Viollet.

Jerusalem: a stony city upon a stony hill. Its venerable melée of levels, minarets, domes and flat, blocky walls rises from a landscape that is monotonous, harsh and bare. The land is dry and often sterile, an intense land, a bony and thorny land demanding strength in return for the strength it offers. Jerusalem has endured and withstood pillage, burning, defacement and even reconstruction under the empires of the Assyrians, Babylonians, Persians, Greeks, Romans, Turks and modern states. The Acropolis seems youthful in comparison; Jerusalem seems not to have grown old but always to have been as ancient as the rock upon which it stands and from which it is built.

For all its confusion, Jerusalem is a regal city, regal not with the pomp of the world but with the absolute regality of enduring time and a single, enduring God. Jerusalem is holy for the Jew, the Christian and the Moslem, the three issues of Abraham united in the infinite concept of a single Supreme Being even when they have denied this unity in wars, quarrels and persecution.

The severity and monotony of the land have explained for some writers why monotheistic religions developed there. In sparkling Greece, the variety of a beautiful world and the variety and joy of man's experience within it engendered a variety of gods, each one ready to be courted or placated by men who, having invested them with the strengths and foibles they knew in themselves, were so self-assured that they even dared play one of their gods against another.

But how could gods like these, born to the diversions and intrigues of Olympus, be conceived or exist in the jagged deserts of the Biblical prophets? The sameness of things was harmonious only with the idea of a single God ; the harshness of life demanded that this God be all-powerful, a God Whose wisdom is beyond man's understanding, but of Whose needful mercy he could be assured. This God was not to be bargained with ; His wrath was as terrible as His mercy was great.

In this crossroads of faiths the central spot holy to three great monotheistic religions is the rock accepted as the one on which Abraham would have sacrificed his son had not Jehovah stayed his hand, and from which Mohammed is said to have mounted to the sky. It is protected now by the blue ceramic dome of the Mosque of Omar, erected in the seventh century by the Moslems. Is the rock beneath the heavenly dome really Abraham's rock? The Biblical past is increasingly determined by archæology and scholarship, where it was formerly evoked by faithful association. The Church of the Holy Sepulcher, the Mount of Olives, Golgotha, Rachel's Tomb, the Wailing Wall—as sites, structures or the remains of structures their precise identification is legitimized more by centuries of worshipful acceptance than by irrefutable factual proof. We know that Jesus was born and walked and died in this land, but Jerusalem the ancient stony city is not Jerusalem the Golden that centuries of imagined Jerusalems have created.

Italian. Mantegna. The city of Jerusalem,
detail from "Christ in the garden of Olives."
Panel of a polyptych painted for the Church of san Zeno.
in Verona 1456-1459.
Musée de Tours. *Giraudon.*

The "Dome of the Rock" or the Mosque
of Omar, erected over the sacred
rock wich had been the base for
the sacrificial altar of the
Temple of Solomon. Ommiad Dynasty
7th century.
W. K. Müller-Atlas Photo.

Jerusalem seen as in a dream. Painting by a 12 year-old girl

In the hundreds of Jerusalems painted by artists who have known the city by chancy descriptions and inaccurate records, the dome of the Mosque of Omar has been introduced to make a Jerusalem of an Italian hill town or a French fortified city. The slopes of Jerusalem have accommodated Flemish peasants' huts and have been recognizable as bits of Spain. But this transformation of fact into a vision of faith has its appropriateness, for Jerusalem is everywhere that its God and His prophets have entered our lives.

French. Enguerrand Charonton. The city of
Jerusalem, detail from the "Coronation of the
Virgin." 1454. Hospice de Villeneuve-lès-Avignon. *Giraudon.*

Mecca

The heart of Islam is Mecca, and the heart of Mecca is the Ka'ba, a small cubicle temple covered with black silk which is embroidered, in golden letters, with verses from the Koran. It protects the sacred Black Stone, once white but, Mohammed said, blackened by the sins of men. Before Mohammed, the rock was saved from the deluge by the Angel Gabriel for Ismael, son of Abraham and ancestor of the Arabs. Mecca centers around these austere symbols of a religion founded in austerity, and around the holy wells of Zemzem, which sprang from the desert in order that Ismael should not perish from thirst.

In its less miraculous origins, Mecca grew upon its desolate site at the edge of a rocky desert plateau because it offered a waterhole to slave merchants and caravans carrying the riches of India and China to Byzantium. Mohammed was born there, returned as conqueror, and accomplished, the year before his death, the first pilgrimage, touching the Black Stone. No other place of pilgrimage holds quite the concentrated promise of Mecca: the reward is Paradise for the believer, and by the thousands the believers come to perform the rites that, repeated by the hundreds of thousands of time s have been their own sanctification of the city as a well of faith.

Veiled women on a street in Kabul, capital city of Afghanistan. Islam is not only a religion; it is also a way of life. The 350,000,000 human beings united in observing its customs form a community stretching from the chain of the Atlas Mountains to the Gobi Desert, from the Atlantic to islands of the Indian Ocean. *Unations*.

در حلقهٔ عشق جان فروشم ی حلقه او مبا دکوشم

Persian miniature.
One of the essential rites of a pilgrimage
to Mecca: seven processional
circuits of the Ka'ba.
The Ka'ba, a black cloth-covered cubical
sanctuary, is the chief object of Moslem
pilgrimage to Mecca. Turkish sultans once
sent a new cover each year
by sacred caravan on a richly caparisoned
camel. The old coverings
afforded a revenue to the eunuchs in
charge of the sacred place. The
smallest shred was a costly relic and a
waistcoat of the precious fabric was
supposed to make the wearer invulnerable
and was a fit present for a prince.
Bibliothèque Nationale, Paris.

Burmese. The Buddhist temple of Ananda to the east of the ancient Pagan wall. End of the 11th century. Still in use, it is still the destination of an important pilgrimage. *Guy Lavaud.*

The five thousand temples of Pagan, the religious capital of Burma, inhabit the landscape like repetitions of a thought timelessly held and timelessly pondered. Architecturally they are variations of the type-monument of Buddhism, as the colonnaded sanctuary is the type-monument of ancient Greece, or the Gothic cathedral of mystical Christianity. The bulbous domes are those of the stupa, a funerary monument under which the dying Buddha asked that his disciples place his ashes, and the conical peaks that pierce them are the form of the royal parasol, symbolizing at once the axis of the world and the center of the celestial sphere. Merging with traditional forms of the Brahman temple, dedicated to Buddha and the Brahman divinities, the monuments of Pagan are deserted and in ruins after a thousand years. But rising like miraculous growths from an earth dotted with cactus and wild plum, they rebuke the ephemeral reality of the visitor. In their quietness they affirm the power of meditation to release the spirit from what is earthly and conduct it to what is divine, reducing to inconsequence the agitations of the world beyond the horizon.

Statue of the Buddha at Pagan. *Guy Lavaud.*

Pagan. Temple in the form of a Buddhist stupa. 9th-10th centuries. Chinese chronicles of the T'ang Dynasty give us an idea of the prosperity of the Burmese empire in the 9th century and of the opulence of Pagan, its capital. "The wall of the city, sheathed in green and shining tiles, measures 160 lis, has twelve portals and a pagoda at each corner. The inhabitants live in houses roofed in lead and zinc. They are Buddhists and worship at hundreds of monasteries with glazed walls and painted with silver and gold, vermilion and other pleasing colors. The floors of these temples are covered with patterned carpets like the residences of kings."
Guy Lavaud.

Pagan, holy city of Burma, seen from the Gawdawpalin temple. *Guy Lavaud.*

Italian. Portrait of Saint Francis of Assisi, the only authenticated one known, painted two years after his death. A fresco in a monastery chapel at Subiaco, near Rome
L. von Matt, Rapho.

The quietest revolution in the history of western consciousness, considering the breadth and the profundity of its effect, must certainly have been St. Francis of Assisi's. The essence of his revolution is that he identified the divine with the natural, making a Christian harmony from elements that Christianity had put in conflict. He was a mystic who loved the world; an ascetic dedicated to the principle of joy; a Christian whose lyrical poems to nature could have been understood, could almost have been written, by pagan worshippers of the sun. He was simultaneously a man of action and a man of contemplation, a man in whom innocence and wisdom were mutually supporting qualities. The basilica dedicated to him, on a spare hillside above a gentle landscape, harmonizes the contradictions of grace and severity, of majesty and intimacy. In art, the transforming spirit that flowed from St. Francis found expression in new pictorial forms, and these, too, are found in his basilica on the frescoed walls.

When St. Francis sang to "my brother the wind and my sister the rain," he released a new sensibility and thereby a new art. The traditional hieratic symbols of Christian art could not express this new relationship with God; they were too reserved, too removed, even too forbidding, to serve as intermediaries between a loving Father and His children. They gave way to humanized images; the visible world with its warmth, light and air entered the world

Assisi. Monastery church of San Francesco. Begun in 1228, two years after the saint's death, it was completed in 1253. The basilica is actually two churches, one on top of the other. It was erected over Saint Francis' tomb, which was discovered in the crypt of the lower church, but not until 1818.
Sougez.

Façade of the upper church at Assisi. This site of a
rebirth of spirituality was an artistic center as well.
Among artists attracted to it was Giotto, one of the
most revolutionary innovators in art history, who set
painting in Italy on a new track. There were 28 frescos
on the nave walls of the upper church which, if
perhaps not his, are closely related to his
finest work. Notable among these scenes from the
life of Saint Francis are the familiar
"Saint Francis Preaching to the Birds" and the less
familiar "Manger of Greccio." Greccio is the small
town where the saint held Mass in a stable on
Christmas Eve in 1223. The use of mangers in
celebration of Christmas is said to date from that
event in that place. *Sougez.*

123

of art first tentatively and then with a rush as artists developed new technical means. The painter Giotto opened the gates, finding nobility in human passion, drama in natural human gestures. He reflected man in a new stature, not as the measure of all things as he had been in Greece, but as the measure of God's love, which was revealed as equal to God's majesty, and greater than His wrath. Free to discard the forms of an aristocratic code of symbols, and to discover spirituality in the commonest things, artists began a tradition of realism that, proliferating in a thousand directions over the next 600 years, accepted the visual world as the unquestioned point of departure.

Italian. Giotto.
Saint Francis Preaching to
the Birds. About 1300.
Louvre, Paris.
Bulloz

IV
THE GREAT THEMES
OF ART

the creation

nature

work and daily life

war and peace

diversions and games

still-life

the mask of the spirit

dream and fantasy

Michelangelo. The Creation of Adam (detail). Fresco in the Sistine Chapel of the Vatican, Rome. *Anderson-Giraudon.*

The Creation is so vast a subject that artists usually settle for treating it as a didactic narrative without philosophical comment. But if it had never been painted except by Michelangelo, the Creation would be one of the great themes of art because of the magnitude of this single interpretation.

The climax of the story as Michelangelo tells it comes within a fraction of an inch of space between the fingertip of God and the fingertip of Adam, the first electric with life and the second lifted uncertainly and with effort as if it were still heavy with clay and reluctant to receive the divine spark.

Italian. Michelangelo. God Separating the Waters from the Earth.—The Creation of Adam.—The Creation of Eve.—The Temptation and the Fall. Frescos from the Sistine Chapel of the Vatican, Rome. (1509-1511) *Anderson-Giraudon.*

The creation

Michelangelo was one of the few artists of inexplicable power who deserve the loosely used appellation of genius. Like other geniuses, he transmuted his personal response to the time and place in which he lived into timeless and universal terms. Each time and place generates its own style ; style seems to be born through artists by their special capacity to distill it from the air they and their contemporaries breathe. Michelangelo's "style," although the word sounds trivial when applied to him, was appropriate to a Rome swollen with aggrandizement by force and dedicated to the flesh. In his followers the style became merely coarse, violent and bloated ; in Michelangelo it originated as an expression of the terribleness of a world where the sublime is fettered by its coexistence with materiality. He sings the glory of the flesh against a counterpoint of anguish of the spirit, and the glory of the spirit against a counterpoint of the restraining weight of the flesh.

The theme is both elevated and somber—so somber that in organizing it on the Sistine ceiling Michelangelo leavened it with an accompanying series of ornamental figures of male nudes jubilant with youth, who affirm through their vitality the continuing potential of the gift God made to Adam. This gift was more than a matter of a beating heart and the power of movement, which He equally gave to the animals. If the figure of Adam in the great climactic panel were replaced by that of an animal, the anticlimax would be close to sacrilege or farce. The spark that Adam is about to receive is the spark of spiritual awareness, a spark that carries with it the compulsion to investigate and then explain, to wonder and then imagine. These are the impulses that force men to create, and if they do not quite make him a god, at least they give him his arts and separate him from the animals to make him a man.

Nature

The artist confronted by nature is part scientist and part mystic. At one pole is Dürer drawing the hare, and recording with zoological accuracy a thousand details to capture the essence of one small creature. At the other is Sesshû, who believes that the essence of a landscape including sky, mountains, foliage, houses, water and boats is best distilled in a few brush strokes, probably fewer than the number of lines Dürer spent in enumerating the hare's whiskers. In varying proportions and innumerable manners artists combine these methods. As scientists they are fascinated by the structure of things— by bone and muscles ; by the way rivers cut through hills ; by root systems and the growth patterns of branches ; by the flatness of ponds and the turbulence of seas ; by the differing shapes of clouds ; by the way a twig grows from a branch and a forest grows from a hill ; by air bubbles the size of a bead and by cosmological space.

They are fascinated by man-made nature as well—the paths worn through woods, the cities clustered on hills or sown on the plains, the bridges stretched across rivers and the boats that are as natural to water as if they were floating plants. As philosophers or mystics they may try to unify all these phenomena logically or ally them with emotions and states of mind. In his notebooks Leonardo da Vinci correlated the patterns of air currents, flowing water, and curling hair, and he invented landscapes fantastic in effect yet where mountains were formed in accord with the processes of geology, storms were bred according to physical laws, and cities disposed themselves in the way real ones grow over the years. He even managed to suggest the staggering extension of nature, in two directions, that has taken place in our century. In one direction we have explored the atom, discovering that a pinpoint may hold its own universes ; in another we have begun to explore universal space, reducing our planet to a pinpoint whirling in one of an infinite number of systems.

This double consciousness on either side of the visible world may explain why landscape and animals occupy so much smaller a part of artists' interest today than in the past. The details of the earth, which have seemed so significant and enchanting to artists for centuries, now seem of less consequence in the disturbing complexity of which they are such tiny fractions. Yet Picasso

Japanese. Sesshu (1420-1507). Landscape Ink wash. Seattle Art Museum.—Sesshu, one of Japan's greatest painters, was influenced, as were all of his artist contemporaries, by the lyrical monochrome landscape style that originated in the Ch'an (Japanese: Zen) monasteries of South China in the Southern Sung Dynasty and he made inspired, individual use of it. He incorporated into his never-never settings exaggerated patterns of dramatically abrupt, lightning-sharp brushstrokes. These reflect Sesshu's discipleship of Zen, the dominant Buddhist sect and the anti-logical philosophy that teaches the practice of an intuitive striking through into awareness as the means of attaining the "enlightenment" the Buddha had found *Giraudon.*

Inca. Head of a puma. Kero (wooden vase). Resin enamel finish. Region of Cuzco (Peru). Possibly 16th century. Musée de l'Homme, Paris.

can still produce a wildly humorous and faintly sinister goat that is at home with a puma's head from Incan Peru, a group of deer from 17th century Japan, a bizarre fish from ancient Persia, a hippopotamus from the Egypt of 5,000 years ago, a bull from the half-legendary world of Crete. It is an extraordinary creature, as convincingly constructed, in its own way, as Dürer's hare, and the more goaty for exaggerations and violations that defy zoology. Its closest relatives are far away in time and cultures, in spite of its modernity; it has cousins-once-removed among the medieval beasts that symbolized the vices, the virtues, and the human temperaments, and it has half-brothers wherever tribal artists have made masks or fetishes from animal forms.

The common denominator in all art based on the theme of nature is that men, animals and landscape are fellow participants in a meaningful universe. In the simple fact of its existence, nature may be meaningless, but we have never been able to accept this appalling idea because, after all, we are part of it. There must never have been a time when men have not identified the changes of season with the cycle of their own lives from birth to death, and it is impossible for us not to think of "nature's moods" even if we reject the cliché and even though we know that moods have nothing to do with the operation of the weather. Artists think the same way, and in their responses to nature they have echoed our ways of comprehending the world about us, or shown us new ones, which in either case means that they have assured us that we have a secure place in the scheme of things.

The tender world of Corot; the pulsating world of Van Gogh; the jagged world of Picasso; Courbet's sea, a sea to feel, to plunge into, a sensuous sea; Klee's city on two hills, an enigma disguised as a simplification; Cézanne's vibrant but neatly joined valley; Mondrian's tree that merges its pattern with patterned space; all of these are personal visions, sometimes seeming to refute one another, often contrary to our way of seeing, but for that reason extending our experience. Art offers us every attitude toward nature except the impossible one—indifference. Existing unexplained, and renewing itself inexplicably, nature has always been our incontrovertible assurance that the mere fact that life exists must mean that it exists toward some purpose.

French. Léger. The Builders
(on yellow background).
Tapestry. 1950.
Marc Vaux.

Persistently the daily tasks that keep the world in running order have turned up as subjects for painting and sculpture. But for thousands of years they and the men who do them were shown only as auxiliary to the cults of gods, rulers and heroes. Men learned slowly to understand the dignity of work that has nothing to do with anything regal or anything supernatural; hence artists were slow to discover it as a theme.

True, some of the liveliest and most engaging sculpture of ancient Egypt shows slaves and common people at work—boatmen, bakers, harvesters, manual laborers. But these are incidental subjects related to the glorification of the Pharaoh-god and to his service, usually created only to be buried with him as proxies for the real thing. The artists of classical antiquity showed us shepherds and vineyardmen going about their work gracefully in idyllic settings, but they were not human beings with lives of their own; they were props in the décor of poeticized landscape. With the beginning of a Christian art, the same laborers were idealized as religious symbols; the laborers in the vineyard became the workers for the church, and the pastoral guardian became the spiritual protector, the Good Shepherd. They still were not ordinary people doing ordinary things.

When the philosophers of the Middle Ages codified the universe into one vast symbolical unit, every activity of man was knit into the scheme. In the divinely supervised cycle of the seasons under the ordained rotation of the stars, each month had its special activity, including so unspiritual a one as hog butchering. Thus man's work took on dignity by divine association, and his labors were represented in the sculpture of the cathedrals along with the miraculous events of the Bible story. But if you had spoken to a medieval man about the inherent dignity of toil, all religious associations aside, the chances are that he would have thought you were propounding a puzzle, a foolishness, or a heresy.

When the daily life of common people began to appear in art as an independent subject of some consequence, it slipped in by the back door of the picturesque or the humorous. There were exceptions, like Bruegel, who recognized the earthy vitality of peasants as something significant in itself

French. Courbet. The Stonebreakers.
1849. Private collection.

French. Daumier. Washer-
woman. 1861. Louvre, Paris.

Mesopotamian. Woman spinning. Relief.
1st millennium B.C. Louvre, Paris.

French. Gromaire.
The Reaper. 1924.

Work and daily life

beneath the clownishness and the grotesquerie that even he often capitalized upon. And certain Dutch painters in the 17th century discovered that very pleasant pictures could be made showing women going about household tasks. It was the same century in which we have seen Le Nain painting simple people with a new respect, indicating the stirring of a new consciousness.

It not only stirred, it exploded in the 18th century with the French and American revolutions, but in the meanwhile the labors of men received their most bizarre interpretation. Court painters showed shepherds and shepherdesses in dainty silks and satins, a mode so pleasing to Marie Antoinette that she herself played shepherdess on occasion in the appropriate setting of a chic little mill built to her order.

One would have thought that with the revolutions achieved, art would have burst into a glorification of the daily tasks of the populace. But the tradition of elegance and oratory was so strong that painters coasted on it, especially since the prosperous bourgeoisie who were art's new patrons were more ambitious to identify themselves with fashion than with the substrata from which they had risen. As late as 1849 they were shocked when Courbet painted his "Stonebreakers," and they passed by paintings like Daumier's deeply reverent "Washwoman" leading her child by the hand, for sentimentalized pictures of mothers and children devoid of all true warmth and humanity.

But a world transformed by the industrial revolution offered new aspects too fascinating for the artist to ignore. And a social system in which the

Mexican. Rivera. Sugar Cane. 1931. Philadelphia Museum of Art.

Dutch. Van Gogh. The Reaper (after Millet). 1889. Stedelijk Museum, Amsterdam.

Greek. Hellenistic. A town crier. Terracotta.

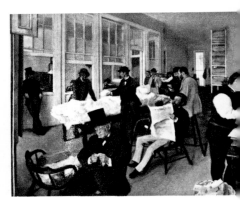

French. Degas. Portraits in an Office. 1873. Musée de Pau.

French. Villon. Orly. 1954. Collection Galerie Louis Carré, Paris.

common man was increasingly the strongest force demanded its interpretation in art, which must draw its nourishment from the forces that
determine the character of a civilization. In France the everyday world
triumphed in the art of the impressionists, so that Degas could paint
the clerks and buyers in a cotton broker's office as legitimately as
Raphael once painted congregations of saints, and Monet could paint the
St. Lazare station as a kind of temple to a modern god, Energy. Art has
served politics and social theory, as it does in the murals of Diego Rivera,
but its discovery of the everyday world is, in the end, another proof
that art's first function is lyrical and interpretative. For Léger the work-
men on girders are not social entities but elements in a pattern reflect-
ing the sleekness of mechanized life. And Villon's airport of Le Bourget,
continuing the idea of Monet's railway station, abstracts from a merely
useful collection of buildings a crystalline essence of a contemporary
world where man extends his environment not by magic, but by science.

French, Monet. La gare Saint-Lazare.
1877. Louvre, Paris.

139

War and peace

War may be the most lamentable of our group sins, and artists in recent times have said so. Goya in his "Horrors of War" and Picasso in his "Guernica" have shown war as the brutalization of innocent victims. But the historical truth is that artists have seen war as horror only when they were on the losing side, as Goya and Picasso were in these instances. Victory makes war in retrospect seem a noble adventure in which right has triumphed, and wars seen as history become spectacles of high drama in which we are audiences and not participants. This is so true that for ages men regarded the warrior as the supreme hero, and war could be celebrated as a function of the glorification of the state. This attitude inspired Greek sculptors to magnificent sculpture on temples; inspired Roman sculptors to representations of war as the richest pageants of all; produced medieval manuscript illuminations in which war became an aristocratic joust. The Renaissance continued these traditions, and the ultimate picturization of war as the great spectacle is Altdorfer's "Battle of Alexander," where a tempestuous universe joins company with multitudinous armies on a scale that eliminates all consideration of destruction, and where suffering is unimaginable as part of a spectacularly organized fantasy. Such records neither offend nor appall nor warn; they cannot, since they are not, in truth, records of war or even glorifications of war,

but rather glorifications of a vital force in a state of magnificent eruption. And since victories are more often celebrated than defeats, this force is usually presented as triumphant in the service of good over the power of evil. But this is a tradition that had already run so thin in the early nineteenth century that paintings celebrating Napoleonic victories are only windy. And in the twentieth century, a century of wars, no painting glorifying war or seeing it as a pageant has approached "Guernica" with its opposing statement.

Column of Trajan in Rome. White Carrara marble. Height of relief band, about 50 inches. A.D. 106-113. In terms of the number of figures, 1500, and the concentrated fullness of the story they enact, this was the most ambitious frieze composition attempted up to that time in the ancient world. The column celebrates and chronicles, in all meanings of the term "epic proportions," Trajan's victorious campaigns against the Dacians (the ancient inhabitants of Romania). Its great height (125 feet, including the base) was topped by a statue of the Emperor knocked down and destroyed during the barbarian invasion of Rome in the Middle Ages and replaced by order of Pope Sixtus V in 1587 with the statue of Saint Peter which crowns it today. The base holds the Emperor's ashes in a golden urn. The continuous spiral of the relief band which circles the column 23 times would, if unwound, be 656 feet long. Rich in detail, it could tell us more than any book about the arms, war machines, costumes, flags, encampments and trophies of Trojan's exploits, but it is impossible to read above the fourth or fifth turn. Even to follow the story that far one must, as a scholar has described it, "run around in circles like a circus horse." The scholar who quoted this wonders "for whose benefit the elaborate pictorial account was intended." He points out that in Roman times the monument formed the center of a small court flanked by public buildings at least two stories tall but doesn't consider this an answer to his query. Just to look at the column, however, convinces us of the grandeur of the Rome in which and of which Tacitus wrote. *Elliot Erwitt. Magnum.*

German. Altdorfer. The Battle of Alexander. 1529.
Alte Pinakothek, Munich.

M VLT: SVPERAT
P EDIT :CM.EQVIT
: MATRE·QVOQVE
REGCVM·M·HAVD
A·DILAPSE·CAPTIS.

Norman. The Bayeux Embroidery. Late 11th century. Musée de Bayeux.—Sometimes called a tapestry, this is more accurately described as an embroidered frieze. It unrolls to a length of more than 240 feet although it is a little less than 20 inches high. It is the oldest work known of its kind and has importance as a historical document

help of her ladies in waiting in about 1080, not long after the events it pictures took place.

The events in brief: Harold, brother-in-law of the English King, Edward the Confessor, was shipwrecked on the Norman coast and made prisoner by William who freed him only after he promised that when Edward died he would

ed the building of a fleet (second episode). Sailing across the Channel, he landed at Pevensey (third episode). He made camp at Hastings: battle equipment was organized, tents and kitchens set up and his position fortified (fourth,

because it records happenings preceding the conquest of England by William of Normandy. Using what is to us a familiar comic strip device, it accompanied each "frame" with a Latin inscription explaining and commenting on the action. According to tradition, Matilda, daughter of Baudouin IV and wife of William, embroidered it with the

recognize William as king. The promise was too simple and fortuitous to be kept. Harold persuaded the English nobility and the people to make himself king. The first embroidered episode shows Harold's coronation. From this point on events and their illustration follow in quick succession. William decided to invade England and order-

episode). The last two episodes recount the Battle of Hastings on October 14, 1066, during which Harold met his death. Known as the Conqueror from that day on, William became a king of England.

From time to time art has been called upon to represent the delights of peace in direct contrast with the horrors of war. A notable single example is Lorenzetti's 14th century mural on the walls of the town hall in Siena, where Peace is shown as a goddess draped in classical gauze and surrounded by the results of good government, a reminder to the city fathers that the first obligation of responsible leaders is the good of the people. But Peace usually turns out to be a rather pallid goddess, a wallflower alongside her more highly charged sister, Victory, who is courted by warriors and is, in fact, the daughter of war.

And yet the theme of peace in the broadest sense permeates art to a degree so great that we could risk saying that of all themes it is the dominant one in the complex interweavings and overlappings of spirit that constitute all expression in art. The function of art has been defined as the creation of order from the chaos of human experience. We have seen how artists have ferreted out this order in nature, have found it in the works of man and in his daily life. They find it also in divertissements and games; in the mere existence of inanimate objects; in our inner life over the whole range from anguish to happiness; and in the world of dream and fantasy. The battlefield is the place where temporary conflicts are settled by violence, but art resolves eternal questions by contemplation.

French. Renoir.
Child Drawing. 1888.
Private collection.

Italian. Campigli.
La Scala, Milan. 1951.
Estorick Collection, London.

French. Robert Delaunay.
Footrace. 1926.
Private collection, Paris.

French. Douanier Rousseau.
Père Juniet's Cart. 1908.
Private collection, Paris.

People are not always free to choose the work they do, but they make their own pleasures. Hence our diversions and our games may say more about us than our jobs do. They are a release of impulses created by needs that lie close to the sources of our lives, and their apparently superficial nature is not superficial at all. The Greeks made athletic contests a part of religious observance, and the ceremonies of our churches today can be traced to popular theatrical spectacles where men found illumination through entertainment. In its own way the theater remains a form of ritual, and children's games are rituals invented in innocence of what ritual means. The set patterns of ring-around-a-rosie or of London Bridge give a child all the satisfactions of a formal ceremony, and the accompanying songs or rhymes are a kind of incantation.

The Sunday stroll in the park and the family outing in a vehicle are forms of communion with nature, which, although we no longer court it with magic, we continue to revere with affection stirred by responses as old as human consciousness. The artist finds all these activities worth recording because, whether he stops to think in such terms or not, he recognizes them as expressions of what we believe in and live for. They offer him, too, fresh color and warm vivacity for translation into painting and sculpture where the human body assumes characteristic expressive attitudes—whether the concentration of gesture in Renoir's " Child Drawing" or the curious distortions of Fazzini's "Gymnast"—and where the human setting ranges from trees and skies to operas and night clubs.

Italian. Fazzini.
Gymnast. Bronze. 1948.

French. De Staël. Jazz Musicians; in memory of Sidney Bechet. 1952. Private collection, Paris.

Spanish. Zurbaran. Lemons,
Oranges and Rose. 1633. Private
collection, Florence.
Giraudon.

"Still-life" is one of the most perspicuous terms in the vocabulary of art, although we ordinarily use it without thinking of how wonderfully compact and descriptive it is. In two syllables it says that inanimate objects have their own vitality, whether they are fruits and flowers that have grown in nature, or plates and pitchers fashioned from inert earth. The French call this kind of painting "nature morte," dead nature, in an exceptional failure to invent an appropriate designation.

Still-life painting can, of course, be deadly. It has been much abused by artists with no skill except a mechanical facility in the imitation of the surfaces of things. The trained hand in the service of nothing more than a photographic eye merely embalms objects in pigment, giving us substitutes for objects we would prefer to have around to touch, to smell, to use, or to see with a completeness impossible in the single aspect offered by an imitative painting. At best, this kind of painting may give us the valid but fractional pleasure of watching a bright technician perform his tricks.

Then what is the appeal of still-life? It offers artists the perfect subject for working out problems that might still be called technical ones but go beyond

French. Matisse.
Ink drawing. 1941.

manual control, problems involving the calculation of pictorial patterns from random material and entering the area of creation through expressive modifications of familiar trivia. Zurbaran's manipulation of light reveals forms, colors and textures in a pattern of balances that has its own abstract beauty independent of the represented objects. Going a step further in dealing with much the same set of objects, Cézanne tilts and warps them out of normal perspective in a scheme of balances and counterbalances that invests his still-lifes with the flux and balance of all nature. His distortions forecast Braque's cubist analysis of form where the objects all but disappear. The change may seem extreme, but when we look back from Braque's abstraction to Chardin's realistic still-life of objects resting quietly on a shelf, we see that neither painting is "natural." Both are carefully analyzed arrangements of form. The Chardin tells fully only when we recognize its mastery in the disposition of static masses, its harmony of light and textures, that account for its revelation of the honest life inherent in simple things.

French. Cézanne. Milk Pitcher and Fruit on a Table. 1888-1890. National Museum, Oslo.

French. Léger. Kitchen Table. 1925.

French. Gauguin. The Ham, 1889. Phillips Collection, Washington.

French. Braque. Musical Instruments. 1911. Musée d'Art Moderne, Paris.

Dutch. De Heem. (1606-1683-84). Lobster and Fruit. Toledo (Ohio) Museum of Art.

Italian. Crespi (Lo Spagnolo). Library Shelves. 1715. Bologna.

French. Chardin. Still life with pipe. After 1756. Louvre, Paris.

Italian. Caravaggio. Basket. 1596.

149

French. Seurat.
The Artist's Mother. Crayon.
About 1883. Metropolitan
Museum, New York.

The artist's achievement in revealing the spirit behind the mask of the face is more complex than we realize. He cannot assume, as people have a way of doing, that features offer a code for deciphering a personality—that small eyes close together indicate craftiness, that the fullness of the lips is a measure of sensuality, that a short turned-up nose must go with an impish temperament, just as a long, drooping one is the badge of melancholy. If such dubious generalities could be applied with any consistency—if we could judge a man by the sum of his features—then there have been humanitarians who should have been thugs, thugs who should have been ascetic prophets, ascetic prophets who should have been tyrants, and tyrants who should have been great humanitarians. Michelangelo should have been a beggar, and Rembrandt a clown.

We are closer to truth when we say that as a face ages it becomes a record of experience. Yet it is more true that time is unselective in distributing its alterations; it collapses and discolors the flesh of an old monk, an old storekeeper or an old actor with equal indifference and in much the same way. We may deduce from dependable clues whether an old face has been weathered

French. Rouault. The Apprentice (detail).
About 1925. Musée d'Art Moderne, Paris.

Italian. Carpaccio. Portrait of a Man (detail).
About 1490. Museo Correr, Venice.

The mask of the spirit

outdoors or protected indoors, whether its owner has smiled more or frowned more. But we are on shaky grounds when we deduce from a set of features that the owner has been kind or cruel, honest or false. Even facial expressions are only partially revealing: does the look of extreme concentration on the face of a stranger who passes us on the street come from the singlemindedness with which he is planning a murder, pondering a mathematical theorem, or trying to remember a shopping list ?

Nothing but long acquaintance with a face, with its repertory of expression, can make it an affirmation of the character we have come to know behind it. But we think of every face as the focus and the sum of a personality. The artist's problem is this: if a portrait is to be more than an objective record or a piece of flattery—in other words, if it is to be a work of art— the inner person must be revealed through features that may belie it. And since shifts and changes of mood are impossible, everything must be told through a single, static, painted mask. The artist must discover the nuance of expression, the one tilt of the head, that says most. He must emphasize here, or subdue there, this detail or that detail which tells truly or falsely. But this is only a beginning. There are less apparent but more powerful devices. The artist's

Italian. Leonardo da Vinci. Saint Anne, detail from the "Virgin and Child with Saint Anne." 1506. Louvre, Paris.

Italian. Filippino Lippi. About 1459-1504. Portrait of an Old Man (detail). Fresco. An early work. Uffizi, Florence.

Spanish. Picasso. Weeping Woman
Roland Penrose Collection, London.
Painted in 1937 when Spain was
in the throes of civil war,
this face shares the anguish of the
"Guernica" and depicts the
limits of human suffering
with rending violence.

French. Zadkine
(born in Russia).
Bronze monument
commemorating the destruction
of Rotterdam
by German bombs in May, 1940.
A municipal commission,
it was cast in 1954
and now stands in a square
of the rebuilt city.
Marc Vaux.

152

line may be soft or crisp, as is expressively appropriate, his color heightened or subdued. He interprets and reveals not so much through the look of the sitter as through the look of his own art.

When an artist invents a face (just as when he invents a figure) he may depend almost totally on such abstract elements as the gentle modulations of one form into the next which account for the mystical serenity of Leonardo's St. Anne. The tense lines and surfaces of Botticelli's "Entombment" are abstractions, as well as representations, of a grief that is saved from hysteria by the leash of reverence. And Picasso's violent dislocations of form in "Weeping Woman" are only an extension, in a furiously discordant key, of the same process—the shaping of visible surfaces to accord with inner forces.

Dream and fantasy

Modern psychology has taught us that dreams are not visited upon us by mischievous sprites, malevolent demons or guardian angels who steal in while we are asleep, but are messages we send to ourselves, messages we would refuse to accept while awake. In effect, artists have always known this, or at least have practiced a kind of exploration with a cousinship to dream. The artist is always busy probing to discover what lies beneath the face values that most of us accept without question. So, with his sensitivities ranging beneath this usual calloused surface awareness, it is not surprising that he sometimes probes deeply enough to bring up a fragment of what we call the subconscious. And we unconsciously recognize that the artist works in an area connected with the older idea of dream when we speak of "inspiration." The theological definition of inspiration is "a supernatural influence which qualifies men to receive and communicate divine truth," which overlaps the definition directly applicable to art, "the awakening, quickening of creative impulse as manifested in high artistic achievement."

For sensitivities attuned to this impulse there is a natural step from lyrical landscape to Van Gogh's "Starry Night," a visionary explosion of universal energy; from dramatic story-telling to Lucas van Leyden's nightmare destruction of Sodom and Gomorrah; from an understanding of the wondrous structure of birds, beasts and mechanical contraptions to Bosch's fantastical aeronauts in "The Temptation of St. Anthony." Chirico, sensible to the peacefulness of small town squares in Italy, shifts easily into an other-world of sinister enchantment; Chagall expresses the heady transports of love by showing a happy couple embracing literally in the air. Bruegel's "Tower of Babel" and Piranesi's imagined prison interiors turn engineering into fantasy, and Giacometti engineers spectral forms into a structure defining the mystery of a dream.

This capacity to define and hold what is ordinarily vague and elusive is the contradiction and the power of visionary and fantastic art. "He who does not imagine in stronger and better lineaments and in stronger and better light than his perishing and mortal eye can see," said William Blake, "does not imagine at all."

154

5

6

7

8

9

11

Dutch. Vermeer. The Artist in His Studio. About 1665. Kunsthistorisches Museum, Vienna.

V
THE ARTIST
AND HIS WORK

talent

method

abstraction

13 years old.—Dürer.
Self-portrait. 1484.
Albertina, Vienna.

Contrary to popular assumption, talent is not a rare commodity. It is only as rare, at any rate, as adaptable intelligence. There is an even chance that the majority of painters and sculptors became artists because their interest was attracted and their intelligence channeled at a time when the twig is bent, and that they would have been just as good, and just as happy, in some other way of life if chance had bent it in another direction. The young child is interested in everything; all objects come to him as total phenomena and he explores everything with random and indiscriminate jubilance. What is a bird? The way a child first comes to know a bird may be one of the thousand reasons that combine to make him a veterinarian, a biologist, or a flight engineer.

A crayon is a phenomenon that you can take in your hand for making marks on things, and colors are wonderful. The discovery that he can make pictures comes to a child later than the discovery that he can walk, but just as naturally. He may live very intensely in this picture-making, and if he is left to himself he works with a spontaneity that adult artists may envy. He does not compare his work with other pictures, and to try to teach him the rules of drawing is as wrong as to try to teach him ballet while he is still crawling.

17 years old.—Raphael.
The Three Graces. About 1500.
Musée Condé, Chantilly.

15 years old.—Toulouse-Lautrec.
Gunner and Two Horses. 1879.
Musée d'Albi.

162

15 years old.—Michelangelo.
Combat of Centaurs and
Lapiths. About 1490.
Museo Buonarroti, Florence·

His absorption in picture-making and his production of estheti-
cally appealing accidents is often mistaken for talent. But
talent, in the form of continued absorption supported by such
physical equipment as is prerequisite (a clear eye and a coor-
dinated hand for the painter, a true ear for the musician) is apparent only with the approach of adolescence, when the personality
begins to coalesce through selections and rejections of interests
and the examination of ideas, all affected by a turbulent gush
of new emotions. This is the age when the potential artist can
learn the techniques that discipline childhood's instinctive
expression, the time when, in the past, the boy would be appren-
ticed to a master artist if he was not, as so frequently happened,
already under the tutelage of a father or relative. He is quick
to learn his teacher's formulas, but as he masters them he is
also quick to discover where they fail to serve him.

The rest of the story that turns the adequate technician into
the true artist is the story of the individual's maturing. Whether
he becomes a great artist or a minor one is a matter of what
kind of person he becomes and of how successful he may be in
developing for himself the forms (as different as Michelangelo's
and Botticelli's) that are the best vocabulary for what he has
to say. There is nothing very mystical in this process, in spite
of the fact that artists hold a special position as spokesmen
for so many intangibles. But there is something close to mystical
in the capacity of intelligence to absorb the experience of the
world and to translate it into any form that clarifies or intensifies it.
And beyond talent there is genius, which in art is possibly the
unimpeded development of an acute intelligence supported by
extraordinary physical aptitude for a particular kind of perfor-
mance. If the explanation seems too mundane for something
usually called inexplicable, then we can only fall back upon the
explanation that genius is God-given.

18 years old.—Velasquez.
The Old Cook. 1617. National
Gallery of Scotland, Edinburgh.

12 years old.—Picasso.
Study of a nude.
1892-1893. Crayon.

23 years old.—Delacroix.
Dante and Virgil in Hell. 1821.
Louvre, Paris.

French. Rodin. Statue of Balzac. Final version. Bronze. 1891-1898.—It was seven years before Rodin delivered the portrait of Balzac ordered by the "Société des Gens de Lettres." He worked longer on this piece of sculpture than on any other. The purpose of the commission was to pay homage to the man who had written "La Comédie Humaine" and Rodin wanted to fashion a likeness of the author that would also express the feeling he had for this monumental accomplishment. With the notion of capturing the look of Balzac at work, of recreating a boisterous and impetuous person who was at the same time an impractical idealist, the sculptor hunted out all the still-living friends of his literary hero. He thought of forming a body that would evoke an epic and of giving it Balzac's head. He blocked out nudes, using as model a peasant of a type he looked for and found in the author's birthplace. His friends thought the results exactly what he must have been aiming for, but Rodin was not satisfied. After several tries he abandoned the idea of a nude; it seemed inadequate, belittling and out of date. Finally he had the inspiration to use the old homespun dressing gown Balzac had always worn when he was writing, to make of the body enveloped in it a shapeless mass, heavy with the potential of unformed ideas, and to give it a masterful, triumphant head.
Sougez, Edit. Tel.

Method

A technical virtuoso may dash off a painting in the way an acrobat performs a stunt, and with less effort, but like the acrobat he may give us nothing more than the spectacle of a brilliant display of specialized agility. By a defective syllogism this could mean that all quickly executed art is attractive but trivial. Yet Rembrandt could make a notation of a few broken lines and say more about an expanse of countryside than some artists who have belabored the details of a single landscape composition for years. Ingres, who was as meticulous a draughtsman as ever lived, said that an artist should be able to draw a workman falling off a roof in the time it took him to hit the ground. Rodin, whose struggle to say what he wanted in one statue is demonstrated on these pages, could sometimes say what he wanted in a few bits of clay thumbed into shape while a model walked around the studio. By what rules does an artist work? By none, by many, by a set that he is always testing and changing. He is free to do anything except settle for less than he knows he can give. In a sketch he must be as decisive as in an elaborated work; the most carefully analyzed work must be as alive as a sketch. There is no contradiction here, since the goal is the same: to bring form and statement into a single identity. Rodin's series of studies for his monument to Balzac show the sculptor changing forms drastically as he widens his conception. Cézanne's variations on his theme of cardplayers show him studying the ways in which a set of forms may be disposed and redisposed in architectural balance. The progressive stages of Matisse's "Rumanian Blouse" are the record of the gestation of a pattern.

Rodin. Studies for the Balzac statue made between 1892 and 1896. *Archives photographiques, Paris.*

French. Cézanne. The Card Players. 1890-1892. Courtauld Institute, London.—The artist made studies of the subjects for this theme in various positions and compositions. Some were sketches, some completed paintings. It has never been determined in what order they were made. *Giraudon.*

Cézanne. Study for the player on the right in the Courtauld Institute version. Watercolor.

Cézanne. Pencil study. Museum Boymans-Van Beuningen, Rotterdam.

Cézanne. The Card Players. 1890-1892. Barnes Foundation, Merion, Pennsylvania.

Method

Cézanne. The Card Players.
1890-1892. Collection Pellerin,
Paris. *Bulloz.*

Cézanne. The Card Players. 1890-1892.
Stephen C. Clark Collection,
New York. *Bulloz.*

Cézanne. The Smoker. Study
in oils. 1890-1892. Private
collection. *Bernheim-Jeune.*

Method

French. Matisse. The Roumanian Blouse. May 1940. Musée d'Art Moderne, Paris.—The process of the creation of a work of art is a mystery. Steps of the process are illustrated below and we can study them endlessly trying to find a clue. These are selections from a fascinating series of photographs taken of a work in progress from the first rough sketch in December 1939 to the painting the artist accepted as satisfying in May, 1940.

Abstraction

In the first picture discussed in this book we saw Whistler insisting on the abstract elements in his portrait of his mother by calling it "Arrangement in Gray and Black." Today Whistler would probably have joined the abstract movement, and would be painting exquisitely arranged gray and black rectangles without identities as a wall, a curtain, a floor, or an old lady. The terms "non-objective," "non-figurative" and others have been coined to distinguish totally abstract work from work that is partially abstract to any degree except the ultimate one. But we will use "abstract art" here to mean contemporary art that rejects reference to objects and deals only in pure forms, shapes, colors, lines, textures and the other elements that we have already seen as the artist's vocabulary. The difference is that the abstract artist no longer uses this vocabulary for description, not even for interpretative description, as artists did in the past.

Art does not have to be abstract to be contemporary in spirit, but since abstraction as a movement is peculiar to the 20th century, it is usually called the art of our time. Historically its appearance seems to have been inevitable. The omnipresence of photographs surely has much to do with the painter's loss of interest in representational images in our century, but all during the 19th century there were forecasts of abstraction. Turner in England and Monet in France shattered form and color to the point of abstraction; Cézanne abandoned realistic perspective, light and shade, and other devices of conventional representation.

In talking about nature as a theme of art we said that science had expanded nature in two directions—into the atom, and into the universe. A man does not have to be a scientist to have his way of thinking transformed by such discoveries. The change is in the air, and our consciousness that the physical universe is made up of infinitely more than the eye can see has contributed to the artist's distraction from the visible world. Abstract art is full of instances where invented forms resemble those in microphotographs, in graphs of mathematical formulas, or in other scientific documents that put the invisible physical world into visible terms.

Abstract art may have developed, too, because easy travel, hundreds of

Abstraction

museums and millions of books have made art from all times and all places accessible. The effect on the artist is double: on one hand he discovers art's illimitable range; on the other he feels hobbled because everything seems to have been done. He becomes fascinated by the widest general principles of art, but hypersensitive about applying them in manners that have been used before. Abstraction affords an opportunity to apply the principles in their purity, while its rejection of reference to nature makes it a new manner.

As a single example, we may recall the painting on page 129, by the Buddhist monk Sesshû, whose summary of a landscape in a few quick strokes applies the Zen principle of reducing to a minimum the interval that separates inspiration from execution. The same principle is involved in one form of abstraction called "action painting" in which the artist may literally fling the paint onto the canvas. Of all forms of contemporary art it can be the silliest when prostituted, but Jackson Pollock's "Number 5, 1948," facing this page, is a legitimate example. The title is essentially a filing number, deliberately bare of any clues to subject or mood, insisting that art is something with an independent existence—independent, that is, from any idea that created forms must originate in familiar ones. And yet two familiar aspects of nature in the accompanying photographs, one of snow on branches and the other of the shadow of a tree on a wall, are suggestive, in the first case, of the heavy skeins of paint that weave through "Number 5, 1948" and, in the second, of the painting's flickering, shifting effect. The comparison is valuable if it helps us to recognize the quality of growth and energy that unites the painting in a funda-

Snow on branches. *Brihat, Rapho.*

Plane tree shadow on a wall. *Kardas.*

American. Jackson Pollock.
Number 5. 1948.
Alfonso A. Ossorio and
Edward Dragon Collection.

Abstraction

mental way to nature, or rather to the life that charges nature. But it is a dangerous comparison if it leads us to hunt out representational elements in the painting the way a child likes to find the shapes of animals and people in clouds. Clouds are most beautiful in their own right; the shapes they take on have their own abstract beauty as pure forms, as well as another kind of beauty as visible expressions of the dynamism of sun, wind and water that has formed them. Similarly the painting is most beautiful just as a painting, and even as the record of the dynamic gestures of the skilled and imaginative artist who flung, dripped and splashed the paint onto the panel, and of the weight and fluidity of the pigment itself, which was allowed to play its own part in determining the shapes of the skeins as they fell. Many associations are possible. Some people like to humanize a Pollock of this type by regarding it as a kind of symbolic map or web of the movements of people in their chance encounters with thousands of other people in the crowded and hectic contemporary world. Others have liked to see an imaginary chart of the tracks of atoms spinning and careening in space. In the most general way such associations have their validity, but when they become specific they limit or distort a painting that, in the end, must exist simply as itself.

This existence is very real, for reasons that cannot be suggested by a color reproduc-

172

Ploughed fields seen from a plane. *Doisneau, Rapho.*

Microphotograph of crystals. *Widmayer.*

tion at reduced size. A painting like "Number 5, 1948" is a compelling presence in a room, not only because of its vivid color, its kinetic pattern and its great size (it is eight feet high) but for a reason peculiar to abstract art. We might say that each bit of paint, whether a gobbet or a wide trail, is "life-size" and hence a presence in a room just as a life-size portrait is likely to be more a presence than is a small one. But "life-size" is inaccurate, or incomplete. Each bit of paint in the Pollock is an actuality in itself; it is not a life-size replica of something else, but something that exists nowhere else, in no other form, than in the unique form we see when we face the painting. This can still be true, although less emphatic, of the forms in abstract painting where the pigment is smoothly applied.

Complicated or inconsequential as this may sound when it comes as a new idea, it brings us to the point where we must say that abstract art, although opposed to what we call realism, has its own special kind of reality. This reality is most inevitable in abstract sculpture, where "abstract" can be only a relative term. Wood, stone and metal are just about as tangible as anything can get. If we have already said of the "Winged Victory" that its "clinging and flying drapery is realistic in effect, but actually an arbitrary, even abstract, sculptural pattern," we can say much the same thing in reverse of another flying form, Brancusi's

"Bird." This piece of gleaming bronze is an arbitrary, abstract sculptural pattern, not intended to resemble a bird, but it is as real, and in its way as alive, as any bird that might by chance perch upon its tip.

By all of this we seem to be on the verge of saying that there is no essential difference between abstract art and representational art, and up to a point this is true, depending on what you mean by "essential." Both kinds of art offer the esthetic pleasures of form, color, and the rest of what we have called a vocabulary. In abstract art these pleasures may be more intense because they must be more pure, unalloyed by all the preconceptions that affect our way of seeing a painting or a sculpture representing something recognizable from other experience. The worm in this apple is that these preconceptions may be necessary as a point of departure for comprehending what the artist wants to tell, if art is to mean anything much to very many people. The abstract artist sacrifices this advantage—or more often regards it as a hindrance—and hence is often left talking to himself or to a very small company. After half a century of abstract art, people still complain of its lack of communication and, while admitting its visual appeal, insist that it is only decoration and says nothing.

The truth is, of course, that anything we find decorative, if we do not tire of it, is likely to be appealing to us for deeper reasons than we recognize. There can be a kind of communication between a vase and its owner, although the owner has never thought of it that way and has never stopped to think that a vase is a kind of abstract sculpture. But the strongest argument for the validity of abstract art is that it has endured attacks that began fifty years ago and has found a constantly widening audience. Some people point out that a malevolent virus may spread in the same way, and it is true that opportunism, fashion, and some artists' inability to cope with tradiional ways of expression have given us a flood of abstract pseudo-art. But one of the happiest circumstances proved by the history of art is that good art tends to endure and bad art tends to disappear. This winnowing is already taking place as today's art becomes yesterday's, and we will see. We will see.

French
Manessier.
Salve Regina. 1945
Musée des
Beaux-Arts, Nantes.

The printing of the heliogravure and letterpress for this book was completed in August, 1962 by the Imprimeries de Bobigny (Illustration and Sapho type combined). The blocks for the coloured plates and book jacket were engraved by Clichés-Union and printed by the Imprimerie J.-M. Monnier, Paris. Binding: Prache, de Franclieu et Cie, Paris, France.